D1109596

This is a photograph of Zachary, an ethereal being from a star system known as the Pleiades. Janis Abriel took this photograph of Zachary in Aspen, Colorado in August of 1995.

The tube of light in which Zachary is standing is literally a vehicle created from energy and light derived from higher consciousness. These vehicles/tubes of light can be used to travel through time, dimension, and space. Entities who travel this way do so in ethereal bodies. At the base of Zachary's shadow, you can see a long, clear projectile. This is a perfectly clear, refined crystal, which Zachary programs with his thoughts to take him to his destinations.

Zachary is referred to in this book as a "Transcendent" because his consciousness and abilities transcend our earthly awareness. Please join Zachary, other Transcendents, and Janis Abriel as they take you on a journey into alternative realities and prepare you for EXCHANGING REALITIES.

Exchanging Realities

A True Spiritual Adventure

In this book, the Creator tells us . . .

You are that part of me that was my heart and my soul, and I wanted to share existence with you in the grandest way, in the grandest scheme of things . . . the experience of differences . . . the experience of so many different opportunities . . . the experience of so many different insights, foresights, and putting-it-togetherness.

And, I sent out my heart and my soul — YOU — in many different forms, on many roads, and in many directions to experience.

YOU ARE MY FOOTSTEPS

This book is an opportunity for you to experience an uncommon journey into awareness on your eternal path of evolution. The spiritual principles in this book are appropriate to our present time and space. They will evolve with you through the dimensions of consciousness.

Exchanging Realities

A True Spiritual Adventure

JANIS ABRIEL

Abriel
Publications

LAS VEGAS, NV

Published by Abriel Publications

If you are unable to order this book from your local
bookseller, you may order directly from
Abriel Publications
Las Vegas, NV
Call: (800) 787-2013 (access code 02)
Internet: http://www.spiritual-endeavors.org/abriel
E-Mail: abriel@earthling.net

Jacket design by Master Makers, Las Vegas, NV
Front cover photograph by Lynne M. Farris, Denver, CO
Illustrations by Laura Zollar of Zollar Design, Las Vegas, NV
Back cover photograph by Theodore Marienthal, Las Vegas, NV

ISBN 0-9667700-0-5
Library of Congress 98-74465

Printed in the United States of America
on recycled paper

First Edition

DEDICATION

The process of creation always involves a variety of hearts and hands. So it is with this book. There are those who inspired it, those who guided it, and those who undertook the responsibility of moral and logistical support.

First, I would like to thank my biological family for the insight and memories they have bestowed upon me. That part of them that has proven to be the greatest part of this book, however, is their acceptance. It is not an easy thing to learn that the biological being you have been associated with from her birth or from your birth has undergone a soul exchange. So, many thanks to my parents for their understanding.

Understanding came particularly easy for my son and daughter. They never questioned my sanity — probably because our love for each other has been strong and accepting from the beginning. To these two beautiful people, whom I love more than words can express, I dedicate my life and many pages in this book to our memories.

Someday, in my own cosmic native tongue, which I forgot in coming here, I'm sure I will find the words to thank Michael for helping me to fulfill this part of my mission. Michael's belief in this book, as well as his heroic support and editorial assistance, were vital to the completion of this book.

I would not have been here to write this book were it not for the cosmic forces that birthed me into this existence in 1987 and guided me every inch of the way to putting this book in your hands. Were it not for their extraordinary wisdom and unconditional love, there would be no book. It is The Transcendents who have breathed life into these pages with their hearts, their minds, and their channeled words.

And, to the Starseed, who come here from other planets star systems, galaxies, and universes to offer their selfless help . . . who bring to the Earth advanced forms of healing, technology, balanced energy, and overall greater awareness . . . and, in particular, to the Starseed who have been meeting with me to nourish our individual and collective spiritual consciousness, and whose questions, insight, and support are an integral part of this book . . . to all of you, I dedicate MY service.

TABLE OF CONTENTS

INTRODUCTION

While my name is on the cover of this book, I can't really take credit for it. Nor can I claim to be a "quick study,"

 having developed the book overnight as the result of an extraordinary revelation. The fact is, I've been working on this book for a very long time. I must even admit to "lifetimes" of preparation.

Nevertheless, this book is timely . . . thanks to those you will come to know in this book as the Transcendents.

It is the Transcendents' ethereal hands which have been lending us assistance from the inception of our humanness. We have called them angels, spirits, extraterrestrials, and even gods. Whatever our name for them, they are an active presence in all of our lives, particularly now. As we prepare to usher in the heralded twenty-first century and wave goodbye to life as we know it, their involvement with us is increasing and evolving. What you will find in this book is a declaration of that evolution . . . much of it in their own words.

Their words frankly address the Earth's foreshadowed and imminent **TRANSITION** into the next dimension of consciousness. They will talk you through the many changes you will be experiencing, the concerns you will be facing, and the how-to of exchanging realities.

This book is the Transcendents' testimony to the power of thought, differences, acceptance, no-limitations, no-judgment, and no-fear. It is their intention to motivate you to live beyond your means — beyond everyday frustrations, misunderstandings, and demands — so you will be prepared to step out into the Universe and meet your brothers and sisters in the sky.

Appropriately so, the first page of this book boasts a photograph of the magnificent Transcendent known as Zachary. This photograph is confirmation that civilizations exist that transcend the human level of understanding and activity . . . that, as you become part of this BIG PICTURE in the Universe when you TRANSITION into the next dimension, you too will learn to travel through time, dimension, and space in "tubes of light" of your own powerful creation. For, when it is time for you to meet your brothers and sisters in the sky, you can move into the Universe in vehicles created by the power of your own magnificent thoughts. When you do, you will leave man-made mechanical devices in the dust behind you.

Yes, I guarantee you that this is so! And, this book is your tool for creating your own such vehicle.

Now, I'm going to tell you something that seems totally absurd. Your vehicle will cost you nothing in terms of money. You will not have to lie, steal, or fight to have it. In fact, you may only create this vehicle if you don't do these things.

Would it not be a wonderful opportunity to create this vehicle out of a knowing of your own incredible self-worth and having acquaintance with those things of existence that bring you meaning, joy, and peace of mind . . . that set aside negative thoughts, attitudes, and actions . . . that guarantee you will never again have to look anger, hatred, or violence in the face?

If you think this is not possible, you are mistaken!

As you've probably already guessed, this book was not written to be usual, either in content or format. The basis of this book is my own autobiography. It does not begin when my body began in 1949. It begins when my life began in 1987 . . . a life, that by most interpretations, is not usual either. Whether you believe my story or not is not important. What I have learned is.

I encourage you to hear the words of the Transcendents that I have included in the book. They have earned that name because they have transcended, through hard work, the negativity you know only so well. I have learned from them more about love, peace of mind, and meaningful existence than I ever thought was possible. Through our talks together and our travels into other dimensions and times, they have instilled in me confidence in existence. I no longer need hope. I have knowing. Now, I won't settle for less.

Nor should you!

In reading this book, you will become familiar with the three extraordinary, transcendent beings who have guided my experiences and my words. It was actually at their direction that I undertook this project. I will share with you now, in their words, what this book is about.

"The theme of the book is reality . . . that reality exists wherever one may go upon the Earth, on other planets, in other star systems, even in other galaxies and universes . . . and, that the differences in realities are the beauties in existence . . . and that the more beautiful we want our reality to be, the more beautiful it shall be."

"The things that we've spoken of to you — creating one's own reality, the power of thought, the power of differences, the importance of no expectations, no limitations, no judgment — these are the things that should come out of the book."

"It should make people long to know more, particularly of those things of beauty, consciousness, and higher ideals . . . a motivation to transcend violence and to move into the Universe in vehicles of higher consciousness. Use these words, 'MOVE INTO THE UNIVERSE IN VEHICLES OF HIGHER CONSCIOUSNESS.' Here is the purpose of the picture of Zachary we gifted to you — to show that this can be done."

The Transcendents

This book was designed with two formats. It is a true story . . . an autobiography . . . an adventure . . . a spiritual adventure. It is also a spiritual handbook. As a handbook, specific spiritual topics (entitled Channelings) follow each chapter of my autobiography. **THESE CHANNELINGS EXPLAIN HOW AND WHY SUCH AN EXTRAORDINARY ADVENTURE IS POSSIBLE.** This "channeled" information came from the Transcendents — beings whose intellectual and spiritual aptitudes transcend those of our own here on the Earth. For that reason, this information may challenge your own personal beliefs, religious upbringing, or system of spiritual existence. It is not the intent of these transcendent beings to negate your positive beliefs. Rather, they wish to share information with you that expands and builds upon your present thinking. Their words are filled with options for greater awareness and, consequently, greater joy in living.

I received this channeled information from the Transcendents in an "altered state of consciousness." Basically, that means I didn't use my human brain. Instead, I accessed the "supraconscious" abilities of my immortal soul — what others in our Universe call the LIFE FORCE.

Much of the channeled information in this book was communicated at meetings of a spiritual support group I started for people the Transcendents call Starseed. Starseed are human beings whose life forces are not native to the Earth. Unlike Earthean life forces, the life forces of the Starseed come from other planets, star systems, galaxies, and even other universes with a specific mission to help the Earth and its human inhabitants. You will be introduced to some of these Starseed in the book and have the opportunity to learn about the cultures and beings from their various cosmic origins.

During the course of each Starseed meeting, the group members asked questions of the Transcendents relevant to an assigned topic on **PRACTICAL SPIRITUALITY**. It is my sincere desire that the questions and topics of the channeled information will have relevance to your own life, sparking insights that will bring you meaning and peace.

The chapters which tell the story of my own spiritual adventure talk about many of the people who have played important parts in that story. Some of these people have been given pseudo-names to afford them the respect of anonymity.

As you read this book, you may find there are words and concepts you are not familiar with. To assist you in understanding these words and concepts, I have included a **COSMIC DICTIONARY** at the back of the book. This Cosmic Dictionary, in and of itself, is a warehouse of information. I encourage you to refer to it often and become familiar with the concepts contained therein to assist you in accompanying me in this **TRUE SPIRITUAL ADVENTURE**.

In all fairness and a desire for you to truly enjoy this book, I must warn you of its eccentricity. You will, no doubt, find yourself expecting this story to unfold chronologically. Alas, I just couldn't get it to follow that conformity no matter how much I tried. So, I conceded to a universal euphemism, "Existence is a space out of time." Therefore, you will derive your greatest pleasure and understanding from this book by experiencing each chapter as a unique and complete space out of time. What I'm trying to say is that you will find each chapter has its own particular theme. I hope you savor each one.

As you read this book, some of you may find yourselves wondering if it isn't really just another product of a mind geared to science fiction. I must admit, if I were you and reading this for the first time, that might be my impression. Now let's turn the tables — pretend you're me: *You're not reading it. You're writing it because you lived it. You're still living it. This is* YOUR *reality.*

Truth is stranger than fiction, for sure.

I would like to reiterate why I'm risking your doubt and ridicule to share this with you. Simply, I want to share the joy that living this spiritual adventure has brought me. I've learned through these experiences and through the thousands of consultations I've had with my clients that meaning in our lives comes from knowing who we REALLY are. We know we have parents, maybe even brothers and sisters, aunts and uncles, and others we share human genetics with. But, do you know that you have an extended family out there in your Universe? You may even come from "out there" like I do. Wouldn't you want to know if you did?

Even if you don't come from "out there," you still share a lively existence with us every day. We are all in this together. To remember together, to grow together, to love together, and move into the Universe together.

As you read this book, do yourself a simple favor. Just ask yourself, **"WHAT IF?"**

". . . But Yesman, WHERE do I find this thing
you call truth?"

"Everywhere you go."

"And WHO will show me what it looks like?"

"Everyone you meet."

"And HOW shall I benefit from what I find?"

"You will find yourself."

Zachary

Janis Abriel
October 1998

THE EXCHANGE

I looked down at Cassy's human body as she lay sleeping on the bed. Zachary, my father, and Zachariah, my uncle, were with me. I turned to their ethereal forms and smiled. The time had come. This was the culmination of two-and-a-half years of preparation, both on Cassy's part and mine.

We had become very close, Cassy and I, during those two-and-a-half years. As I became familiar with her "Earth" memories, life style, ambitions, family, and body, she was practicing letting go of them. We had spent much time together in the ethereal realms talking and working through each other's concerns, preparing for this very moment. She was ready now to RETURN to her cosmic home in the Pleiades, and it was time for me to LEAVE my cosmic home in the Pleiades and with "The Command" to begin my mission on Earth.

I entered Cassy's body. In our practice sessions, our life forces had traded places. She would leave when I would arrive, and I would leave when she would arrive. This time, our life forces joined. I felt the energy of my life force melt like butter into Cassy's. It was a cosmic experience in a human body. We became one with one another and with her body. I looked up from the bed and saw Zachariah lift his arms. They turned into magnificent white wings. He scooped our human body up and cradled us in his wings. Then we took to flight through the cosmos in bubbles of light . . . Zachary, Zachariah, Cassy, and I. It was magnificent!

As we moved through the heavens, I wanted to reach out and touch the stars. There were millions of them, bright in a dark blue sky. Though we were moving through this celestial wonderland at warp speed, I felt entirely peaceful and safe, like a child in Disney's Magical Kingdom.

It took very little time for us to arrive at our destination. It was so large, I first thought it was a planet. Then I realized it was a city in the sky — The Command's mother ship. Zachariah carried Cassy and I into a room and laid us on a crystal table. My life force left Cassy's body, and I joined mother, father, Zachariah, and my twin sister, Alcion, on one side of the table. Cassy's Pleiadian mother was standing on the other side of the table. Zachariah grinned at me and laughed. "Do you think your uncle has lost his mind, bringing you here like this on wings?"

"Never," I replied. "It was a glorious gift and an unforgettable farewell."

Cassy shivered on the crystal table. The table sensed she was cold and surrounded her in warmth. It then sensed and responded to her other needs to feel comfortable and safe. After a while, when she felt the time was appropriate, her own life force left her body. She was greeted and welcomed back to the ethereal realms by her Pleiadian mother. Immediately, the table surrounded her physical body in a cocoon of energy to preserve its integrity and ensure no loss of body functions.

It was time! For all of my existence in Pleiades with mother, father, and my seven brothers and sisters, I had been taught to be of service to the Universe and to the Earth. In earlier times, I had occasion to walk on the Earth with your ancestors to learn of your ways. For the last two-and-a-half years, since Cassy's decision to return early to Pleiades, I had worked diligently with my mentor, "She Who Sees Most," to prepare myself for my mission to Earth.

I said good-bye to my family. Then, as I turned to the body on the table, I saw my cosmic companion in the shadows across the room. For the first time, I experienced apprehension. He made no effort to move from the shadows. He knew how difficult this parting was for me. So, we communicated empathically from a distance. As the sobs rose in my chest and the tears rolled from my eyes, I told him I couldn't leave him. He assured me I could.

"No, I can't leave you," I responded. My ethereal body shook as I spoke the words to his heart and mind.

"Yes, you can. You've prepared for this mission and you can do it." His words conveyed confidence to my heart. I smiled at him and entered the body on the table. The next thing I remember is that I was lying on my back in the grass. Above me, I saw a space ship ascending into the sky. I was on Earth in a human body.

I had exchanged realities!

NOTE: As explained more fully in the "Introduction," the "channeled" information that follows each chapter comes from enlightened beings from another dimension of consciousness.   The format of the channelings is question-and-answer. The questions came from people like you. This is so you will be able to relate to the information being shared with you. Because the intellectual and spiritual aptitudes of these enlightened beings transcend those of our own here on Earth, EACH CHANNELING WILL HELP YOU UNDERSTAND MORE FULLY THE SPIRITUAL ADVENTURE IN THE CHAPTER THAT PRECEDES IT.

Enjoy!

CHANNELING

The Reality of Reality

Q. What is meant by the term "reality?"

Reality is allowing yourself to experience and BE everything that you can create and everything anyone else can create.

In reality, there is no judgment. For one to experience the depth of reality, one cannot judge one's reality. One cannot judge one's experiences. To discern and learn from experiences is different than judging them.

The less fear you have, the broader the scope of reality you will experience. For those who are fearful, their reality is very narrow. It is as though they walk along a pencil. For others, reality is a mountainside. For others, reality is a cloud, a limitless expanse. It's whatever you choose it to be. The key to experiencing the most of ALL THAT IS, is to let go of fear.

Q. Is it possible in the third dimensional Earth existence to experience other realities? If so, how?

Absolutely! You already do that in your dream state. Also, understand that most of you are in your mind, so to speak, only ten to twenty percent of the time. So, your third dimensional existence is one in which you only really exist ten to twenty percent of the time. What do you think happens to you the other eighty to ninety percent of the time? You are someplace else. You're just not CONSCIOUSLY aware of it. Let go of fear, judgment, and grief, and you will bring these things to your CONSCIOUS mind.

Q. How does the power of thought affect our ability to experience other realities?

It is the power of thought that IS other realities. In fact, thought is a vibration that flows through the Universe. It is on the back of that vibration that you have the capability of experiencing and creating anything your mind can imagine. So, it is on the back of thought that all reality exists. Only by limiting your thoughts do you limit the extension of your reality. Only by the limiting of thought is there fear. So, if you do not limit your thought, there will be no fear . . . and when there is no fear, there is no limitation.

Q. We have been told that thought will inhibit our meditation, which allows us to travel to these other realities. How does this thought that you're referring to differ from this?

Your BRAIN inhibits your ability to connect with other dimensions because it wants to hang on to the third dimensional things — the activities that fuel your survival and your fun. Thought never gets in your way. Thought really takes place when you get past your brain and into that area which you call your Universal Mind.

There is a difference between thought and logic. In your third dimension, you use the process of logic in order to try to understand how to survive and what the purpose of your existence is. Logic is a product of your brain . . . and, it is that which is connected to the brain that limits you in terms of movement within the dimensions.

Thought, on the other hand, is brought to you through the gift of your life force . . . and the gift of your life force connects you to the Universe.

Q. What is the purpose of having more than one reality?

Joy! Would it not be boring to have only one reality? Why limit oneself? Why not experience excitement and adventure? Adventure comes with experiencing new things. The more you have to experience, the more realities you can walk in. The more realities you experience, the greater you become.

Q. *You have taken the channel, Jan, to realities that in the third dimensional Earth existence would seem fictitious or even absurd — wings on a bird a mile wide, a crystal city in the center of the Earth. Do these realities truly exist or were they just for the purpose of teaching understanding?*

Both. Absolutely, they do exist. If she could visualize them, if she could think them, if she could read our thoughts, they're hers. They're her reality. And all the better if they've taught her something. There is no absurdity in the Universe. To call something absurd, is to judge it. Remember, there need not be judgment in reality. Judgment comes from fear.

Q. *Do each of the eight dimensions of our Universe have a different reality? (Note: Our Universe has eight dimensions of consciousness, the eighth dimension being the realm of highest consciousness. The Earth is in the third dimension of consciousness.)*

In the sense that the dimensions are based upon consciousness and consciousness is based upon an understanding of oneself . . . that as each dimension grows upon the other, it has a greater understanding and envelops entities with greater understanding . . . these entities' realities would then be different because their understanding is different, their abilities are different, their desires are different. So, in that way, yes, you can view the different dimensions as having different realities. More so, you can view it as the different dimensions having different CAPABILITIES FOR CREATION of different realities.

Q. Basically, the main challenge of people on Earth is to manifest survival for themselves, and that's what their attention is focused on. I think if people could manifest the material things they need in life, they would put more attention on their spiritual life.

You think too much about survival. Survival has become not only a word, it has become a way of life. If you did not worry so much about survival, it might free up your energy to think of greater things through which you can experience joy, fulfillment, and meaning.

The word "survive" comes with a connotation of fear. Replace that connotation of fear, that word "survive", with the word "joy" . . . "I am here to experience abundant joy." When you truly believe that, you will not have a concern for survival; and all that you need will be in your hands and at your feet.

Q. Isn't this third dimensional Earth existence we live in an illusion?

Everything is an illusion. Reality is an illusion. But it's an illusion that you want to experience. And you can choose to experience that illusion by touching it, smelling it, feeling it, and hearing it in a physical form; or you can choose to experience that same thing by smelling it, touching it, feeling it, and hearing it in your life force. Illusion is reality.

Q. Is there anything else we have not yet asked about the subject of reality that would be appropriate for us to know at this time?

In order for you to be able to use thought processes to experience alternative realities, you need to also work with those things that you call your feelings and emotions. When you let go of the negative human emotions — in particular fear, judgment, and grief — you can focus on UNCONDITIONAL LOVE. The vibration of unconditional love is your connection to the Universe and experiencing extensive realities.

Zachary, Sananda, & Ezekiel

BIRTH

As I lay on the ground, I watched the space ship hover above me. I don't remember if the grass was wet or dry or what the weather was like. I do remember that the ship appeared to be round and that I watched it ascend into the sky. The next thing I remember was lying in Cassy's bed at home. That was October 17, 1987, the first day of my life on Earth. It marked the beginning of my own struggle to remember . . . myself and my mission.

Although I was in a 38-year-old body, I felt like a newborn infant adjusting to its new home and body. I know why infants cry a lot — pure frustration! Adults take their identities for granted, but an infant feels as if everyone is a stranger, including himself. He must become acquainted with his body and teach it to think, move, react, take care of itself, and understand what is going on around it. I was no different. I was just a newborn in an older body.

How could such a thing be? My human brain told me such a thing was impossible, that I must be on the verge of losing my mind. But something else told me that in time my human brain would understand what it could not then grasp. Deep down inside myself I knew that I had walked into that body from somewhere else, and that the life force who was in the body before me had asked me to do so. But how and why? And how was I to function until I found out?

The next few months were filled with incredible confusion and struggle. I had trouble walking, talking and thinking. I was tired and weak all the time. I stood in a grocery store and cried because I couldn't decide between a can of peas and a can of corn. I couldn't listen to music because the vibrations made me nervous and sick. I had constant lucid dreams of flying saucers, extraordinary beings, and contact with other dimensions. I felt displaced and incredibly lonely. I was sorrowful and depressed. Though I was suffering with heart seizures, the doctors could not find anything physically wrong with me. One doctor attributed it to panic attacks. Others gave me nitroglycerine and anti-inflammatories and sent me home to bed. That bed became my sanctuary as I sorted through all the "not-knowing."

In the midst of all of this, Peter, the live-in companion I inherited from Cassy, walked out and left me with two young children — Cassy's ten-year-old son, Jeff, and twelve-year-old daughter, Tracy. Rather than being a burden, those two beautiful young people became my reason for growing stronger. When I had the strength, I would go with them down to the creek and watch them play. We talked about what I could do and what I couldn't do with them and for them. Together we formed a "survival team." I didn't have much strength, but I had a lot of love to give them. In return, they gave me consideration and a reason for living. That became one of the most bonding times we've ever spent together.

When I developed the strength to venture out of the

house, I went to see a psychiatrist. He unwittingly saved my life. Although deep inside I believed that I was a new life force from elsewhere in a mature human body, I could not voice that to him. All he could deal with was what he saw — a woman abandoned by a companion, stressed by her job, unexplainably sick, and very sad. Yet, with his help, I stepped onto the road of recovery. I became stronger physically, mentally, and emotionally. I hung a bookmark on the bathroom mirror that read, "Soon you will be out there dancing." I knew when I could dance again I would be all right.

Now I was motivated . . . and with the help of my new family and friends, I developed the courage to turn every painful movement and activity into an opportunity to overcome my human challenges and become a healthy, stronger human being.

CHANNELING

Mountaintops

"Where are we to go today, father?" I asked Zachary. I had a direction in mind when we started out. But, as usual, I find that Zachary, The Teacher, has already picked the classroom.

"Come with us. We want to show you something . . . something different."

We're standing on a mountaintop. Is it on Earth or someplace else? I can't tell. Zachary says it doesn't matter where it is. The significance of this lesson is that every person's feet are meant to stand on the top of mountains. Every single soul upon the Earth is meant to climb, and overcome, and stand on the top of mountains.

Here is the reality of the third dimension — that every person has the courage and the ability to surmount life's challenges and, then, to stand on top of the third dimensional mountain he has bettered and feel his power.

We should never disempower anyone. For, even those who would appear to be useless, sedentary, or harmful have a purpose, and a meaning, and a direction. It is necessary for them to be here. It is necessary for them to be who they are for themselves, for others, and even for the Universe. For all that transpires upon the Earth affects the Universe, as well. If our hearts could only be softened towards one another — if we could only feel that unconditional love for one another — we would understand.

In the meantime, we can accept the understanding of the Transcendents — WE DON'T EVER STAND ON A MOUNTAINTOP ALONE. We stand on mountaintops always with another or others. For together there is twice the strength. As a species, there is unlimited strength.

Zachary & Janis

BABY STEPS

Cassy's friend, Wendi, picked me up to go dancing — despite my protests. I had been in self-imposed solitary confinement for almost three months. I really wasn't ready to venture out yet, and the night proved to be disastrous. I was still very uncomfortable around people, and I felt like a foreigner in a strange land in the bar scene. My memory banks held stories of my love for music, dancing, and people; but I certainly didn't feel that way this night. I just felt terribly displaced.

As I stand back and view that picture now, the dance was like my first step out of the crib. I have a new-found appreciation for the feathered entities who, under fear of death, learn to use their wings upon their first departure from the nest.

I survived that first step, and the next experiences were not quite as traumatic. An evening with Wendi at the state fair a month later was almost enjoyable.

Some of the other friends Cassy passed on to me were also invaluable during this time. Despite my constant (seemingly absurd) question, "Why do HUMAN BEINGS do that?" they chose to ignore my newfound eccentricity and hung in there with me. (It took me nearly a year and-a-half to substitute the word "people" for "human beings.")

I did feel an immediate connectedness with Stephanie

and Mark, Cassy's New Age friends. They weren't judgmental. They were into higher consciousness, flying saucers, and extraterrestrials. Now, I could relate to that. I didn't know why yet, but I could.

I went to Stephanie and Mark's workshop shortly after my soul exchange experience. I don't even remember now the specific topic. But, suddenly I didn't feel completely alone. Here were other people who had visions. They cared about things of the heart and the spirit. They wanted to know more than the "usual."

I formed my own very first friendship here with a delightful woman named Evlyn. I felt immediately drawn to her ready smile and sweet vibrations. I didn't realize it at the time, but the bond we formed through this workshop would form an alliance that would spur both of our spiritual growth for many years.

That first night at the workshop, as Evlyn and I sat there on the floor and talked about a variety of spiritual and ethereal matters, I found words coming out of my mouth that I had no "reasonable" connection with. I found my own voice within my head asking, "Hey, words, where did you come from?" "No matter," another voice answered, "the information is appropriate. Learn from it as you speak it." And it was appropriate . . . because it felt at peace in my soul.

And I did learn from the words. I also learned to respect and honor the voices that spoke to me and through me. That workshop established my lifeline to my remembrance of myself . . . myself from elsewhere. Though I didn't comprehend it at the time, I was laying the foundation for my understanding of the relationship between the corporeal and ethereal worlds. While most of the people I had "inherited" from Cassy through my soul exchange believed that their identities were in their human bodies, I was beginning to remember otherwise. I started opening up my cosmic memories of the IMMORTAL and ETHEREAL nature of all of existence, including human beings. I started to practice disconnecting my immortal life force from my mortal human body. I discovered that my body could function for a period of time without my life force to activate and preserve it. During those periods of time, my life force was set free to explore other realities.

In the workshop, I traveled to another dimension where I spoke to spiritual forces — evolved souls who shared their transcendent wisdom with me. This process was so easy and natural for me. I felt at home with it. Now I know that was because those other dimensions WERE home to me.

At the workshop, an ethereal owl came from one of those dimensions to become my companion for many years. On its heels, it brought other ethereal winged entities who would swirl around me whispering their approval and other positive affirmations in my ears. I never knew when they would show up. It was always unexpected, during a learning experience of some sort or another. They became like the exclamation point at the end of a sentence, driving the meaning of the experience home.

One evening a few months later, these winged friends

played a special part in a truly extraordinary experience that Evelyn and I shared. We had discovered a "special place" at one of the parks in town. It was a grassy knoll which overlooked a tiny amphitheater on one side and sloped playfully down into a grassy mesa on the other side. One night, after the park was closed and no one else was around, Evlyn and I, my "new" son, Jeff, and his close friend took a blanket to the top of the knoll and lay under the stars pondering the magic of "out there."

Suddenly, I saw a space ship at a distance in the sky. It looked like a large pulsating globe of brilliant light in the darkness, and it moved in a zig-zag pattern above us. Minutes later, its movement halted and a beam of light emanated from the craft directly to us. On the back of these vibrations of light flew hundreds of my winged friends. One, a hummingbird, landed on Evlyn's shoulder and started pecking at her cheek. Evlyn, who had a strong capability for sensing and feeling the ethereal realms, but could not at that time see them, asked me what was pecking her cheek. "Only your favorite bird," I laughed. We all laughed as I described the scene, which now resembled something like an aviary.

"I can see them too!," exclaimed Jeff's friend. There was something else this young boy FELT, as well . . . something I felt so strongly it captivated my complete attention. The vibrations that were being sent from the craft were filled with LOVE . . . love so overwhelming it took my breath away. Now, more words, their words started filling my head. They were words of praise, honor, encouragement . . . words of higher meaning.

These words and the love became the only things I was aware of, the only things I wanted to be aware of. I tried as best as I could to share the words and feelings with the others, but it was impossible to express everything I was hearing and feeling.

We must have been a sight that night . . . laughing, and crying, and dancing on the top of that knoll. I collapsed from sheer delight.

As the Earth dimension welcomed us back and we walked towards the car, Jeff's friend, with eyes glowing and excitement pouring from his voice, said to me, "I NEVER want to forget how I feel right now!" I knew then that this would be a memory that would affect the rest of his life. In the years to come, as I saw this boy turn into a young man and deal with some very tough third dimensional issues, I had confidence that he would make it through all right because of the insights and feelings of love this experience activated in him.

What a gift the Universe shared with us that night! We weren't just four ordinary human beings. We were four spiritual beings worthy of an extraordinary experience. This experience affirmed that our true value extended beyond our appearance, our age, our education, the type of work we did for a living, and our income. This is when I stopped worshiping the *status quo* . . . as it is in the Universe when we communicate ego-lessly, spirit-to-spirit.

CHANNELING

Ego

Q. Would you please give us a definition of "ego."

Ego is a connection. It's a way of communicating one with another. It happens to be just a baser way of communicating. So, in terms of a definition, ego is a form of communication based upon baser, more physical needs than those desires of the life force, of the spirit, of the entity who's escalating.

Many elemental souls work within ego. Many advanced souls, who are filling their cup to the brim with knowledge and understanding, may work within ego also. That is why it is not appropriate to judge people based upon their working out of this space of ego. Ego is just an experience for them. It is their right to have this experience — to fill their cup of knowledge, understanding, and consciousness. So, one is not necessarily a lesser soul for experiencing these things themselves or experiencing them through another person.

Q. Since we live in a third dimensional existence composed of duality, what would be the opposite of ego?

The opposite of ego is ACCEPTANCE. It is being able to look at the king of a country, at an orphan, or at a homeless person and not pass judgement on them for who they appear to be to you, or for what they do not appear to have. What one has is not always obvious. Some of the greatest hearts beat in some of the shabbiest bodies.

Q. How does one overcome the ego trap?

That is a matter of process. The first thing one must do is not to beat oneself up for what appear to be failures or lower activities of consciousness.

ACCEPTANCE OF ONESELF IS THE NUMBER ONE THING — understanding that, regardless of what you have or what you do, you have limitless value within the Universe. With this strength of mind and character, you can step outside of the things that seem to be so valuable to others and walk the path of your life force. You will know you have this strength of mind and character when you are willing to let go of your neediness and pain . . . when you are willing to move on . . . when you recognize that holding on to the negativity only hurts yourself . . . when you experience that feeling of connection with the Universe . . . when you understand that there is more to existence than STUFF . . . when you rise above stuff and don't need it anymore.

Q. We recognize that ego is prevalent in the third dimension. Do any of the entities in the fourth through eighth dimensions function out of ego? If so, why would they do that?

Yes, they do. They do it because they're in the process just like everybody else. Understand that there are many civilizations in the Universe — many, many civilizations in the Universe that know MAINTAINING a place of no-ego is as much a challenge and an opportunity as arriving there.

Experience is something that continues throughout all of the dimensions, and it is possible to fall back into old patterns within the higher realms, just as it is within the third and lower dimensions.

Remember that ego is a vibration. As we grow in consciousness, our vibrations grow higher. But there's still the memory of this place of ego. We never lose that memory. The challenges may be somewhat different if one is in an ethereal body, but there is always the opportunity to step backwards and to work out of a sense of ego.

Zachary, Sananda, & Ezekiel

MEMORIES

Memories are a powerful thing. If we know how to use them, they enrich our lives, and we can dance and play in the positive energies we create with them. Memories are neither good nor bad. By our own choice, we can either use them to build our personal stairway to the Universe or erect bars that confine our attitudes to negativity, whining, and depression. Once we have an experience, which then becomes a memory, our lives are forever changed. We are never static. We don't stand still. Our memories don't allow us to.

When I did my soul exchange with Cassy, I inherited some of her memories. Since then, I've created many of my own. Before our soul exchange, Cassy's memory banks were scanned and evaluated to determine which memories would be useful and which ones were not necessary. The unnecessary ones were purged, the others retained.

The memories that were retained had two purposes. First, they were to assist me in completing some specific tasks for Cassy, such as raising her children to adulthood and resolving other relationships she had started. After this, I would be allowed to use these memories to assist me in completing my own purpose for coming to the Earth.

Initially, I had no emotional connection to these memories. They were just facts. Cassy had been born and raised in Idaho; she had also lived in California and Utah; she had completed two years of college; she had been married for eleven years to Nathan, and they had adopted two children, Tracy and Jeff. After she and Nathan divorced, Cassy was married to Collin for six years. She was a single parent and had a live-in companion named Peter when we did our soul exchange. She was tall and slender with blonde hair and hazel-colored eyes. She supported herself and the children as an administrative assistant, loved to dance, and had "paranormal" abilities of her own.

In fact, since both Cassy and I are from the Pleiadian star system, our paranormal abilities are quite similar. Her memories, therefore, have been extremely valuable to my own purpose here. It is important to understand that everyone on Earth has a connection to information and abilities that transcend the status quo. Some have a greater propensity than others due to abilities they have developed in prior lives and in that space between death and life before they return here. But everyone is connected to a universal system that transcends the knowledge and wisdom we use to barter our everyday existence. The password into this system is "letting go of fear" — fear of ridicule, rejection, failure, success, the unknown, and anything else that compromises positive energy.

Cassy felt instinctively at a very young age that her journey in this lifetime was a spiritual one. She felt as much of a connection to ethereal beings as to human beings. Her first "medium" experience occurred when her grandmother died. Grieving deeply, she called on her grandmother to return.

Immediately, a presence filled the room. Though she could not see the presence, she felt it deeply. It overwhelmed her. For a high schooler to experience such an unexpected response to her anguished request was frightening. So she backed away from her medium abilities for a number of years.

Four years later, on the night of her marriage to Nathan and while driving to their honeymoon destination, a flying saucer appeared just yards away from them. The saucer was metallic and round with lights on the bottom that turned in a circular motion. It hovered over them for a few minutes and then disappeared. While my memory is one that this was an unusual experience, Cassy was not afraid. Frankly, the marriage and honeymoon took precedence in her mind that night. The experience was shared at a family dinner two days later, brushed over, and never discussed again until 1996, twenty-seven years later. It was not until Cassy's and my daughter, Tracy, was married that the memory resurfaced. The night before Tracy's wedding, Nathan asked me if I remembered the flying saucer "we" (he was referring to Cassy, as he was not aware of the soul exchange) saw on our wedding night. He told me that he had always believed the space craft was there that night because it had some connection with me (Cassy).

After her marriage to Nathan, Cassy began to have symbolic dreams that proved to be foreshadowings of events in the lives of her friends. Nathan believed she had no right to these premonitions, so she stopped discussing them. But she couldn't stop the dreams.

Another paranormal ability surfaced spontaneously on an occasion when she was speaking in a church meeting. Cassy experienced an unexpected telepathic connection with a woman from South Africa. She found this woman's voice and mind communicating through her to the congregation and imparting information she was totally unfamiliar with. It was a powerful experience knowing that another entity, voice and all, was speaking through her. This trance channeling, as she later learned it was called, opened her up even more to paranormal possibilities. However, she never shared this experience with Nathan or their friends.

Several years later, after her divorce from Nathan, when his brother lay dying in a hospital many miles away, Cassy re-activated her dormant medium abilities to speak with her dying brother-in-law. She chose, unwittingly, to connect with him just at the point of his passage through the portal of death. His guides through the portal did not want his passage disturbed, so she told them she would "call back later." She never did. The next time a medium connection was made, our soul exchange had been completed.

These are some of the memories I inherited from Cassy. Immediately upon our soul exchange, my own paranormal experiences began. I had spontaneous visions and encounters with entities in the ethereal realms on a daily basis, sometimes many times a day. It was not frightening. In fact, most were quite beautiful. It just wasn't quite understandable . . . yet.

As I began having my own experiences — through day-to-day living and paranormal activities — the memories I inherited from Cassy began metamorphosing from facts to feelings. In fact, my first reaction to my paranormal experiences was to withhold them from others, much as Cassy had. But over time, with the help of Cassy's metaphysical friends, I learned to respect, develop, and use these abilities.

These paranormal abilities have become my vehicle into a world of awareness, multiple dimensions, and past and future times. They have re-connected me to many beautiful entities beyond the Earth — my family and companions in the Universe, who are now my companions, teachers, and confidantes here on Earth. I have experienced a peace beyond all understanding as I've resolved quandaries and questions in alliance with these beautiful transcendent beings. They have guided me wisely and diplomatically as I've worked to overcome my own fears and appreciate the unknown, the unconventional, and the misunderstood.

CHANNELING

Fear

Q. What is the nature of fear?

Fear is much misunderstood. Fear, as with everything in your existence, has a dual nature.

The fear to which you most often relate is the fear which paralyzes and keeps you from moving forward. There is also that fear that propels you, that causes you to reach out and go for more. In that way, fear is appropriate.

When fear brings negative thoughts that cause you negative actions, watch out to avoid it. You are paralyzed and cannot move forward because of the negative energy that surrounds these activities. In these cases, fear can be hostile to your well-being.

Sometimes, however, when you talk about the subject of fear, you shoot from the hip. You choose to say that anything that causes you emotion, particularly negative emotion, is inappropriate. Sometimes those things that bring negative emotion in the third dimension are a necessity because they get you to decline what is in front of your face, push against what exists, and move forward. It compels you to get your fingers dirty digging that tunnel through the mountain so that you have to go only one mile instead of ten in the direction of What Really Is.

Q. What causes fear?

Fear is a by-product, in your HUMAN existence, of the human body. Fear is a product of things working in conjunction with one another — the chemicals in the body and the emotions in the body. Those things come together to create a picture that you can respond to either with fear or love.

Q. Are we born with fear or do we create it?

Both. As you are propelled out of the birth canal, the very shock of exiting that warm, safe, comfortable abode and going into a world in which you experience the cold, bright, strange, different, and indifferent makes one of your first experiences fear. That makes you an expert in carrying it on throughout your life. After that, you are capable of creating it yourself through the by-product of the chemicals and the emotions produced by your body. You re-create fear in different ways with different experiences.

Q. Do we carry fear over from past lifetimes on Earth and/or experiences on other planets and star systems?

You do not carry fear into this existence. Fear is a product of the human body. The life force which comes to that human body has memory of other lifetimes on Earth, on other planets, and in other star systems. Those memories, when keyed, can be responded to in a number of different ways by the human body, including fear.

Q. Is it possible to live in a third dimensional consciousness without fear?

There's a difference between possible and probable. It is possible to raise one's vibrations beyond fear. In order to do that, one must work very, very closely with one's life force.

By raising the vibrations of your life force and focusing on the things of the spirit, you are capable of raising the vibrations of the human body. When you raise the vibrations of your body to a certain point, you can manifest fear-less-ness. That is not an easy thing to do. It requires an understanding of what it is you want to accomplish and a dedication of your life to doing that — a dedication to nurturing your life force as well as, and even more than, your body.

That does not mean that one neglects one's body. It is

very important that the body be healthy because the health of the body has very much to do with the level of one's vibrations. Therefore, it is wise to maintain and keep one's body in a healthy condition, so that as one continues to raise the vibrations of the life force, the vibrations of the body are raised simultaneously.

This dedication to the things that feed the life force and one's consciousness requires dedication to doing the things that help you understand your relationship to the entire Universe. That can be workshops. It can be things such as prayer, meditation, channeling, empathic communications. It can be reading and writing — read of things that other people give to you and write of the things that come from your soul. Write in your journals. This gives you the opportunity to impose enlightenment upon yourself. Do whatever it is that connects you with your life force.

Q. How do we eliminate negative fear from our lives?

Nurture yourself! Your society, your civilization has made you afraid of nurturing yourself. You're told to nurture everybody else, and somehow have the time and energy to survive. You can't grow by neglecting yourself. You can't overcome fear by neglecting yourself. You nurture yourself and, thereby, get beyond fear. That is what you take to other people to nurture them — your fear-less-ness.

Q. *What is the most appropriate way of dealing with relationships in which fear exists?*

First, understand the INTENT of the people in the relationship — what is the intent of the person who is instilling the fear in the relationship? What is the state of existence of the being who is feeling this fear, who is fearing this fear? Then, find out what the lesson is that is to be learned. At that point, one can conquer the fear by detaching oneself from it — awareness is power is detachment.

Q. *When things happen in our lives that are life-changing — when our whole life seems to be in a turmoil — are we just to accept what happens and not have fear?*

Understand that you are here in this third dimensional existence for a purpose. You have a body for a purpose. You have a body that reacts to experiences for a purpose. It is part of the growing curve you experience through this body that these experiences open up your genetic DNA. Ultimately, you will transcend the human body and its fear — and you are capable of doing that within this lifetime.

Fear can be used as a jump-start to greater awareness

and activity. That's all it's necessary for. It becomes a problem only when you hold onto it beyond that, integrating it into your activities, your communications, and your philosophies in a way that does not allow you to go forward in a state of positive thought and being.

If you become caught up in fear, if it goes beyond serving the immediate purpose and becomes a pattern in your life, then you need to look at your motives to determine why you are continuing to manifest this.

Q. I stand to lose my home because of a divorce settlement. Most of the time I can stay above my concerns. But every now and then, I get sucked down into the fear and have to pull myself back up. I'm fearful because I stand to lose a great deal.

Why do you say to yourself that you have a great deal to lose? It's STUFF, and ashes to ashes, dust to dust, it will go. But your life force will continue on beyond that. At issue is the need to be in that anti-matter of your life force and let go of the matter of the human condition — the matter that holds you into what you think you need, but what you really don't. The only thing that matters is what you know about yourself and what you think about yourself. That's all. Nobody can take that from you if you choose not to let them. They can't take that away from you in a divorce decree. Somebody else may walk away with the house, but if you walk away with dignity, you have what matters.

Q. *Sometimes it seems like I really have nothing to fear, and I sit back and ask myself if I should I be worried. Am I just being complacent, or have I moved past the biggest share of fear.*

You're double guessing your progress here. There's a difference between complacency and health. When one is healthy, one has strong muscle tone. When one is complacent, one is usually not thinking, one is usually not learning. It's a "not caring." You never want to get to the point where you don't care. You want to be at the point where you care about the things that matter, the things That Really Are. It's important to be able to detach with muscle tone. What that means is that you still have a connection — a connection with What Really Is — but you're detached from What Really Doesn't Matter. That's not complacency. That's detachment with muscle tone.

Q. *Once in a while, I get angry about the things that have happened to me in the past. Is there something I can do to eliminate my negative feelings?*

Yes. You can say to yourself, "What I am experiencing at

this moment is not What Really Is. Therefore, I may, in all integrity, detach myself from this experience and the negative emotions that go with it. I may be at peace and be detached, and that is appropriate for me."

Zachary, Sananda, & Ezekiel

LEARNING THE LESSON

There is a fine line between genius and insanity and the spiritual and diabolical. Ultimately, however, they all serve the same purpose — as experiences to raise our consciousness, vibrations, and level of joy. This particular experience is one that Cassy left for me to complete.

In 1982, Cassy's second husband of less than a year molested her seven-year-old daughter, Tracy. Like a stone thrown in a pond, this set in motion a cycle of experiences that rippled outward for thirteen years.

Cassy had met Collin at a church dance. At that time, all of her hours were spent either working at her job or as a single mother of five-year-old Tracy and two-year-old Jeff. She didn't take much time to date, so when Collin asked her out she told him no. Undaunted, Collin begged his way into helping decorate her Christmas tree.

Collin had a youthful face, was soft spoken, and was adept in spiritual conversations. He stole Cassy's heart in a very short time, and she agreed to marry him in a small ceremony in her home.

Cassy's love was fast and deep, but Collin's dysfunction ran deeper. When he looked into Cassy's eyes, he was really looking through her at her young daughter. In retrospect, it is apparent that he married her to have access to Tracy. What an irony that he later grew to appreciate, love, and want Cassy in his life. But by then, it was too late.

Cassy's memories of Collin were vivid with acts of deceit, infidelity, and abuse. She grew up in an ultra-conservative family and town. It wasn't in her own being to lie nor to be consciously unkind. She wasn't even familiar with the terms "pedophile" or "incest." Yet, this is the drama she found unfolding around her and her children. When the physical abuse started, she left . . . only to find out the incest had been taking place. The next revelation was that love couldn't cure pedophilia, nothing could. By this time, her life with the children was fraught with loss of dignity. Dealing with the court system, Probation and Parole, the mental hospital, a halfway house, a sex-offenders program, and Collin's family (who blamed her for reporting the crime) wore Cassy out.

What fuels our lives and activities is energy. Cassy's energy tank was on empty. She needed to rest, but there was no relief from the insanity in sight. Nor could she desert her children, whom she loved with all her heart. Through her metaphysical readings, she was aware of the "soul exchange" phenomenon. So, rather than give up completely, she asked her God to let another life force use her body to complete her responsibility to her children so she could rest.

Cassy wasn't consciously aware of her own Pleiadian heritage. But the Council of Elders on Alcyone in the Pleiadian star system was. The responsibility of choosing a replacement was left to them. I was asked by the Council to come here to Earth, fulfill Cassy's responsibilities, and then go about my own mission. That process began on October 17, 1987.

Tracy didn't show negative signs of the incest for seven more years — not until about two years after our soul exchange. Cassy had divorced Collin thirteen months before our soul exchange. Because I had inherited the memories surrounding the incest but hadn't been emotionally connected to the experience myself, I wasn't harboring any pain of my own ... but Tracy's pain was another matter altogether.

At age fourteen, Tracy started having flashbacks of the incest. Like a monster rearing its unsightly head, depression was in our faces twenty-four hours a day for the next seven years. We all suffered from internal bleeding in our life forces. All hell broke loose as she worked through the injustice in her semi-mature teenage mind. Very few days went by in those years without my thinking about Collin, resenting his existence, or just plain hating him.

About June of 1995, like bumping into a ghost in a haunted house, I started seeing Collin's ethereal body standing on the same street corner every day on my way to work. This didn't shock me because I knew by then that the life force is able to leave the human body and that both are capable of functioning separately for a period of time. Given his consistent "appearances," I realized Collin must have had a reason for being there, but I didn't give him a chance to explain. Instead, my daily response to him was, "This town isn't big enough for both of us, so you'll have to leave." He left, but was always there the next day. This continued for about six months.

In January of 1996, I was notified of Collin's death. By now, I was personally involved in "the incest experience." Nevertheless, the news hit me much harder than I expected. When I received his death certificate, I was spontaneously propelled back in time with him to the day of his death. I found my ethereal body standing in the field outside his home watching him. He was holding a gun to the side of his head. I could hear his every thought. I felt his deep despair. He didn't think he had the courage to go through with it. But he felt that he had no option. He argued these two thoughts in his head for some time. Then there was darkness. I experienced his death as though it were my own.

I kept telling myself that my grief was unnecessary. I knew the nobler purpose of death and the grandeur on the other side of the portal of death. But for two days I couldn't eat or sleep. All I could do was cry. I finally picked my head up off the sofa, barely able to see through my swollen eyes. I said, "Collin, I can't do this without you. Help me." There appeared immediately in the room a beautiful white light.

I felt a wave of vibrations sweep through my body. It started at the top of my head and systematically moved its way down through my feet. Relief! I was completely at peace! The vibrations had literally raised my grief to a level of peace. Oh, the inexplicable joy of What Really Is.

I understand now that Collin knew of his pending death, either consciously or subconsciously, in June of 1995, when he started manifesting himself to me. But, why? In October of 1996, in an unexpected and unsolicited meeting, a clairvoyant told me she saw a man with me, a man who had died. She said he wouldn't "go to the Light" because he wouldn't leave me. I knew the time had come to deal with the situation.

My life force went to the astral plane to talk with Collin. Inhabited by entities who refuse to go through the portal of death and into the Light, this is usually not a joyful place. Various characters who refuse to leave the material plane, or who feel they have some manner of "unfinished" business to conclude, walk this plane until someone helps them through the portal. I asked Collin why he was there. He told me that Cassy and Tracy had forgiven him, but I had not. He said that he would not go through the portal into the Light without my forgiveness.

I was almost knocked over by the vibrations from this truth. In that instant of honesty, I was shocked, humbled, and enlightened . . . and by whom? . . . the man who had filled our lives with so much grief . . . the man who had honored our existence by bringing this experience into our lives . . . to TEACH us. What Really Is whispered in my ear, "This was just an experience . . . an experience with the same purpose as all other experiences . . . to help you and yours grow in consciousness and thereby raise your vibrations." Oh, the healing voice of truth!

I knew through my talks with transcendent beings that there is no such thing as judgment in the Universe. I had witnessed the saint and the sinner being welcomed alike as they passed through the portal of death. Before this day, I had taken this understanding into my head. But on this day, I felt it in my heart . . . and it became MY truth. By letting go of my judgment and anger, we could all finally be at peace.

I saw two ethereal beings come to guide Collin through the portal. When he got there, he turned and looked at me. We both smiled. On the other side of the portal, I could see three life forces waiting there to greet him . . . Cassy, Tracy, and Jeff. This lesson was completed.

CHANNELING

Judgment Is A Dead-End Street

Q. You have told the channel, Jan, that humans do not yet have a very well developed ability to be discriminating. Would you tell us what you mean by "being discriminating."

In your world, "being discriminating" actually has two meanings. Oftentimes, you talk about discriminating against one another. This is the opposite of what we would suggest that you do. When we talk about being discriminating, we talk about a HIGHER OBSERVATION. This is not just an observation, as you call it, but a HIGHER observation — opening your eyes and seeing things as they truly are. Do not hide your head in the sand. Hold your head up high with honor and respect for yourself. Then you can have honor and respect for other people when observing what they do.

In observing what another person does, you can determine for yourself if this is an activity, attitude, or philosophy that you want to incorporate into your own life. Ask yourself if it is appropriate for this to become part of your thinking. Is it something that you want to emulate? Or is it something that you choose not to manifest in your life? If the vibrations of that activity don't feel comfortable to you, then you can choose to reject it. This is not a judgement, as you see it. This is being discriminating in terms of whether or not something is appropriate for you.

Q. *What types of situations or problems does this under-developed ability to be discriminating cause us here on Earth?*

Almost all of them. What we see now, in particular, is in those geographical locations where people are hungry and starving. This agony is due to a lack of discriminatory observation on the part of the mass population. Discriminatory observation should be utilized to ensure that your leadership is competent and capable of leading you to a higher order of living. So, ultimately the things that you suffer from in your world — we talk about hunger, about violence, and about not having the understanding, the learning, the knowledge, the information that you want in your life — are due to lack of discriminatory observation either on the part of an individual or the collective group consciousness.

Discriminatory observation is part of the ground work, the jumping off point for eliminating those things that do not manifest happiness and joy in your life.

Q. We have been discussing the difference between being discriminating and being judgmental. Would you share with us your insight on the difference between these two concepts?

Being discriminating is a thing of the life force. Being judgmental is a thing of the human brain. In your realm of existence on Earth, in your third dimensional consciousness, you experience a tremendous amount of judgment and much less of discriminatory observation. This is because you are more in tune with your body and your brain than you are with your life force. Consequently, you let your body and your brain lead your life rather than allowing your life force to do so. (Is this not a sad situation when you consider that your life force is what really fuels your brains and your bodies.)

Would it not be wise to know the workings of the engine in a car? Likewise, is it not wise to know and understand the workings of the engine in your body — that being your life force. If you truly want to begin to understand the difference between being discriminating and being judgmental, make a commitment to yourself to follow the way of your spirit, your life force. Let your brain take comfort in knowing that your life force will sustain it and take care of it. Your body does not need to control existence. It is your life force that brings meaning and joy into your life. Let it be your goal in life to get to know your life force as well as you know your body. When you do, you will truly understand the difference between being discriminating and being judgmental.

Know that judgment brings pain and misunderstanding. It brings on those things that you call negative emotions. It brings on anger. But discriminatory observation brings wisdom. With that comes a higher order of living.

Q. How is it possible to define ourselves without being judgmental. Doesn't having a value system by which to define ourselves require judgment?

In order to have a value system, you need to NOT have judgment. Why? Because the root of judgement is fear. Fear is not reasonable. It arbitrarily eliminates valid options that you could integrate into your value system. So, if you judge the things that occur around you, especially the thoughts that you are UNFAMILIAR with, your value system will be lacking in awareness integral to your growth in consciousness.

On the other hand, by discriminately observing the things that happen around you, you can reasonably determine whether you choose to manifest those things in your own life. There is a great difference. By using that capability of being discriminating, you open yourself up to an infinite value system. By using judgment, you limit your value system.

Q. *You've explained to us before that it can be "taking the higher road" to end a relationship. Doesn't ending a relationship require judgment? Please explain this irony.*

Understanding this "irony" requires an understanding of yourself. That understanding of yourself comes from being able to discriminate between the value an experience has in your life and what you choose to manifest in your life.

The higher road is always knowing oneself and doing what is right for oneself. This is the higher observation that we spoke about — observing yourself, observing others, observing the results of your activities and other's activities . . . be those thoughts, feelings, or actions — then deciding whether they are appropriate in your life. This is not a judgment. It is discriminating between what will help you grow in consciousness and what will not. It is part of knowing yourself.

Q. *Is there anything else that would be appropriate for us to know about these concepts of being discriminating and being judgmental that we have overlooked asking you?*

It really is much more joyful to be discriminating than to be judgmental. The irony is that you often choose to be judgmental and unhappy. Think about this. If you choose to be judgmental and unhappy, where has the power of your thought gone? You have chosen the lesser thought forms by doing this.

Believe in yourselves. You are not victims, and you do not have to settle for less than what you want. Go for the things that are most important to you. Be joyful. Be happy. Choose the higher road of discriminatory observation.

Zachary, Sananda, & Ezekiel

IT'S ALL IN THE VIBRATION

Despite his frequent walks into the murky vibrations of emotional and mental disease, Collin often gazed intently through his window of physical reality at the bright, light vibrations of kindness and higher awareness. He had learned how to astral travel while sitting in jail awaiting trial for the incest. Another inmate taught him the process. Collin found that releasing his life force from his body to investigate the ethereal realms brought him temporary relief from his human afflictions. This made him yearn for continual peace of heart and soul and prompted him to search for What Really Is in the ethereal planes.

After his release from jail and having gone through a sex offenders program, Collin shared something with Cassy that he had learned on his astral travels. It was a seemingly innocuous day in 1986. Cassy had come home from work completely exhausted. She and Collin were still married, but within a few months of separation and divorce. Stress was high, and Cassy's release from the Earth plane was drawing closer.

Cassy had only enough energy left to fall on the bed. She couldn't move. She lay there motionless. Unexpectedly, Collin leaned over her and started touching the aura surrounding her body. With distinct movements of his hands, he pushed all the negative energy in her aura away, bringing her body and life force into balance. Instantly Cassy felt a surge of energy in her body. She concentrated on that FEELING of increased energy. She focused only on the energy. Nothing else existed. She found she could control the energy by the power of her concentration. She could increase it. And the power increased with every passing second. She had become a human generator!

The aura around Cassy's body became brighter. Then it became larger. The more she focused on the energy, the brighter and larger her aura grew. Within minutes, even her body was pure energy — pure bright light. With no boundaries of flesh and blood, only light emanated from her throughout the room. Soon there was ONLY light — no bed, no floor, no ceiling, no walls . . . only light. She existed in the form of pure energy, and so did her surroundings.

Entities began walking in from other dimensions on the back of the energy's vibrations. They came in many forms, from other places and times. They walked around and around her. They helped her release the negative emotion that was tying her to the Earth plane. Her future passage back to Pleiades was laid here through this energy and through the loving hearts that extended themselves from other dimensions.

When she sensed the experience was complete, Cassy released her concentration. She let the energy ebb as she returned to her corporeal form. Her body shook and twitched, as though she had been hit by lightning.

After forty-five minutes, Cassy's body lay still. However, the process was not yet ended. Her vibrations were still enormously high. She stayed home for the next three days and frolicked in those higher vibrations. In that space, she knew ONLY joy and the peace that comes with feeling at one with all of existence. She had experienced that vibration known as UNCONDITIONAL LOVE . . . and nothing she had ever felt or ever dreamed of feeling could compare with it. It was glorious. It was life changing. It was life shaking. She would ride these vibrations back home when our soul exchange was finalized.

UNCONDITIONAL LOVE IS A VIBRATION

Cassy had rejuvenated her life force with this experience. She was strong and aware enough to travel to that dimension and planet from which she had come. She had also prepared her human body . . . so she could leave and I could enter.

CHANNELING

Unconditional Love

Q. What is the nature of unconditional love?

Nature is a good synonym for unconditional love. Nature and nurture walk hand-in-hand. Nature gives life. Nurture maintains it.

Unconditional love gives birth to people, to things, to plants, to animals, to everything you are and to everything that is around you. It gives birth to higher vibrations and, therefore, to higher dimensions. Those things that give birth, that build, and that accomplish what life and existence is all about is what unconditional love is about.

For instance, when two people come together in any type of relationship — it can be an intimate relationship, a work relationship, a friendship — and they give birth to one another in terms of ideas, philosophies, and behaviors that produce higher consciousness, they take their vibrations to a higher plane known as unconditional love.

Unconditional love is giving birth to these higher vibrations every day, many times a day through thoughtful words, words of kindness, words of honor, and words of respect.

Sometimes, however, people lose sight of what is important in relationships. It is not the house. It is not the car. It is not the job, per se, that is important. It is the people who are important — the people's feelings, the people's thoughts, the people's attitudes.

When you bring an attitude or an action to a relationship that takes away honor, that attempts to negate the thoughts or feelings of the other person, you diminish the vibrations of the relationship. Too much of this can bring death and ending to a relationship. You can see this in your divorces.

Violence is rampant among your people. You are even taking the lives of other people. In a way, that literal taking away of the life of another person is a blessing compared to dying inch by inch at the hands of someone who is suppose to respect, honor, and love you. There is much agony, much confusion, much frustration in the hearts of those who are diminished by their loved ones.

HONORING DIFFERENCES is the key to your transformation to the higher dimensions. To do this, you may have to bite your tongue and question your own motives, ideas, philosophies, and intents. It is not an easy thing to honor differences; but because it is not easy, the vibrations grow all the more.

Q. *With all the difficulties you've talked about here, is it actually possible to experience unconditional love on the Earth plane?*

Yes, it is possible to experience unconditional love on the Earth plane — not necessarily easy, but it is possible. There are those who walk amongst you who do manifest this love. You probably wouldn't recognize their names. That is because they don't seek power. They don't seek open honor. They are the people who understand the things that are important in life, and they know that those things have no relationship to control and power.

In comparison to your population, there are a nominal number of these people. But, that's O.K. Those numbers can be expanded if you share your love with one another. So, if you have that propensity for unconditional love, nurture and help other people to develop it as well.

Q. *What is the major block to unconditional love?*

Fear. You fear that if you love another person unconditionally, you somehow give yourself over to that person and lose control of your life. In essence, it's exactly the opposite. By giving yourself to another person, you realize your life.

Q. Is everyone in the higher (fourth through eighth) dimensions capable of unconditional love?

Everyone in those dimensions is capable of unconditional love. However, there are those who choose not to behave in that way. They choose to search for other things. Just as in your society, they may still choose through avarice, through greed, through ego not to use this capacity. But do they have a greater understanding of it? Do they have a greater ability to honor it and to bring it into their lives? Yes, because they have a greater understanding of consciousness in the higher dimensions.

Q. Is it possible to experience unconditional love at all times and with all people?

It is possible. The probabilities are not high, but it is possible.

If you would put as much effort into being unconditionally loving with all people, at all times, in all places as you do into earning a car or buying a house, your society would be much further along. Instead, your energies are being focused on the material things and not on those things that cannot be seen but are of the greatest value.

If people better understood the power of vibration, they

would be putting their energy into unconditional love. But awareness is power, and now you know. Now you have no reason for not working towards that.

Q. Sometimes we seem to confuse other kinds of love — possessive love, jealous love — with unconditional love. What is the difference between these kinds of love?

Unconditional love is mutual honor. It requires negotiation and understanding. It is something that you work for. It means that you communicate, that you talk to one another, that you sit down and work through the things that are important to you, and that you decide how you're going to honor each other's values.

Unconditional love is not something that you demand. It's something that you work to manifest in your life. It's working through and honoring those beautiful differences in one another. It's making a home for yourselves that is nurturing and does not detract from one another.

If there is possessiveness or jealousy in your relationship, ask yourself why it is that the vibrations are not going up. What is it that is keeping the vibrations down at this level? Why is your partner jealous? What are you not honoring in that person so he or she can feel safe, secure, and unconditionally loved? Then your partner, who has that jealousy, selfishness, or possessiveness, as you so put it, can ask himself or herself, "Why do I feel this way? How can we talk this through? How can we better communicate with one another?"

Q. Could you explain how unconditional love feels?

Unconditional love is the crown jewel upon a person's head. It literally opens your crown chakra to the experiences, the thoughts, the feelings, the attitudes, and the ideas of the higher dimensions. When you have EXPERIENCED the raising of your vibrations to the level of unconditional love, you will understand the GREATNESS of the feeling.

Q. When two people feel unconditional love for one another, but that unconditional love is unhealthy, where do you find balance?

Unconditional love is not healthy? There is no such thing as unhealthy love. It's an irony in terms. It's not possible. It's an unhealthy RELATIONSHIP.

When people go into a relationship because they need something, they're not giving unconditional love. If they become obsessive, if they become hurtful, if they become controlling, if they become verbally abusive, it is not unconditional love.

It's also very important to understand that you're here

to have experiences with people, so you can learn and grow. As you work your way up the consciousness ladder by learning and growing through relationships, you get closer to unconditional love.

Q. We hear that people who are loving should never get angry, emotional, or upset. Is that accurate?

Do you remember the story about Jesus — when he walked in on the money changers in the temple and became very angry?

It's a very good story to remember. There are times when one can confront issues, and must confront issues, in a way that honors one's own consciousness. You won't see anger or emotional upset very often in people who exhibit unconditional love. But there may be occasions when that does happen.

Q. When you are at confrontation's door — when someone is in your face and not honoring you, your blood's boiling, and your mind's racing — how do you demonstrate unconditional love?

Perhaps, by changing the semantics. Instead of calling it "confrontation," you could say you're at "negotiation's door." Basically, negotiation is helping the other person understand you in a way that is acceptable to that person. Then the other person can reciprocate the same process with you. The purpose of negotiating is to reach a common understanding.

It is often the nature of the third dimensional creature and of the human body to react in violent, angry ways. The key is to be able to be at the door of negotiation and do it as calmly as possible. Again, this is a growing experience. It is an opportunity for you to find out what it is that's making you WANT to be upset, angry, and to fight this person.

It's the intimidation that makes me angry.

No. The other person may be intimidating you, but what in yourself is letting that person intimidate you? What is deep inside your own self that reacts to that intimidation? There's the key for learning the lesson of the experience and then using the experience to raise your vibrations.

In negotiation it is not necessary to have a loser and a winner. In negotiation both people should win. You live in a society that wants a winner and a loser. You need to get rid of that way of thinking. You need to get rid of those words. There is no such thing as a winner and no such thing as a loser. There are only winners in the universal scheme of things.

Q. When you are at that door of negotiation, and you believe there's nothing more you can do, is it unconditional love to walk away? Or is it unconditional love to press for mutual understanding?

That is the beauty in life — that you get to make those decisions. Each decision must be based upon its own merits and the characteristics of the individuals who are involved.

Is it unconditional love to know that you are not going to be able to live in harmony with somebody and to walk away? Yes! But walk away without diminishing the other person. Understand that the other person has the right, just as you do, to make a decision to believe and behave a certain way. We're all in a state of growth. Every level and every space of growth is beautiful! Whether you're down here or up here, it is all OPPORTUNITY.

There is always a god's god. There is always a rung higher up. The higher up you get, the more you realize that there is no difference between you up here and this one down there. The tool is to honor differences even if you don't agree with them. But that does not bind you into staying in a relationship that does not allow you to grow in vibrations.

Q. Would you comment on achieving unconditional love for oneself?

That is a very good question because until one manifests unconditional love for oneself, one cannot GIVE unconditional love. But you may learn unconditional love from another person. By another person loving you unconditionally, you may learn to love yourself unconditionally.

To learn unconditional love, you must step outside of fear. Step outside of the need to control. Step outside of ego. Unconditional love starts with what you on Earth call self-esteem and self-confidence — lacking unnecessary ego.

Self-esteem is being able to say to yourself, "I'm not perfect, but I'm where I'm suppose to be. I'm more perfect than I was back then. I know more than I did back then. And I honor that in myself. I also honor the weaknesses in myself because they're opportunities to grow. And I need not feel guilty or ashamed of anything that I do, think, or say unless it harms myself or another person."

If what you say or do inflicts harm, then stop and ask yourself, "Why do I have that need to hurt myself? Why do I have that need to hurt another person?" Look at that situation as an opportunity to better understand yourself. There is nothing imperfect about you. There is only perfection in the making. And it's all right to love yourself.

Zachary, Sananda, & Ezekiel

PARENTHOOD

Besides the obvious confusion that resulted from my soul exchange with Cassy, I awoke to the fact that I was a single parent.

Now, I ask you, how does a soul new to the Earth parent a soul with ten or twelve years of Earth experience? I learned very quickly — *you let them help you!* And help me they did, although they weren't aware of just how critical the part was they played in my initiation into this world of third dimensional vibrations and consciousness.

Nevertheless, as the Universe would have it, I inherited two very wise souls as children. At that momentous point in time, Tracy was just twelve years old and Jeff was just ten. Their maturity, no doubt, was derived from surviving the tides of two divorces and a battle with the incest demons, the attention of loving grandparents, their father's concern, and the devotion and hard work of a mother named Cassy.

The first thing Tracy, Jeff, and I discovered together was that I couldn't do a lot for them while I was getting my human feet under me. Cooking was almost impossible for me, because I didn't have enough strength to stand for more than a few minutes at a time. Grocery shopping was something like a side trip to a torture chamber. Once I stood in the vegetable aisle at the grocery store and sobbed because I couldn't decide between a can of peas and a can of corn. Now, that may sound ludicrous to all human beings out there, but where I come from we don't eat peas or corn! So, Peter, Cassy's live-in companion who had chosen to leave at this time, did come back to serve grocery duty; and the children became great little cooks.

Cars are non-existent in my world. Space ships and tubes of light were my preferred form of travel. So, I had to muster up Cassy's memories on driving. I learned that planning a route of travel on roadways was much more difficult than programming a destination on a space ship or through time, dimension, and space. Besides, what little strength I did have wasn't enough to maneuver shifting gears, changing lanes, and thinking like a driver. So, I drove very little, and the children and I spent most of our time at home.

Oddly (perhaps other parents wouldn't see this as odd at all), I discovered I could not tolerate much noise, particularly the music the children listened to. The vibrations were literally painful. At their own suggestion, the children took their radio outside so I could strengthen myself in quieter vibrations. My domestic sanctuary became like a blanket that I surrounded myself in to heal and experience a sense of security.

I also needed sunshine and exercise to balance my body and life force, so the children and I would walk together around the farm on which we lived. We often stopped at a creek, where they would swim and play. Their laughter was the best medicine I could have had. During those first critical months, we formed a bond that would be unbreakable through the years of experiences that lay ahead of us.

It was immediately obvious to me when the soul exchange was completed that I had inherited a body with a painful, chronic disease. In my dimension we do not have corporeal bodies. Therefore, I found it necessary to set about trying to understand this new vehicle in which I had to function and diagnosing what it was that was causing me so much discomfort. After utilizing impersonal "modern" medicine and listening to two years of ego-driven mis-diagnoses, I finally found the needle in the haystack — a rare doctor who was able to accurately diagnose my body as having fibromyalgia.

By this time, Tracy was a teenager and Jeff was peeking through the same doorway. I knew I had come here to succeed. So, to deal with the challenges of their puberty, as well as my own pain and the other symptoms of fibromyalgia, I turned to my consciousness for answers.

I had learned that conventional medicine had too many side-effects. In fact, it was a toss-up as to which was worse, the disease or the side-effects. Alternative healing became my benefactor. Instead of pills, I devoured spiritual philosophies, nutritious food, and herbs. I became a vegetarian. Through an understanding of the connection between emotional dis-ease and its physical manifestation, I started working on the residual emotional memories I had inherited from Cassy and putting them to rest. Meditation, a positive attitude, my talks with transcendent beings, and my travels to other dimensions and times have brought me to a space where I am almost completely symptom-free.

It would be a great oversight not to mention my beloved cosmic uncle, Zachariah, here. Zachariah became my personal physician. He led me to the information I needed, soothed my suffering brow, and whispered encouragement in my ears. Some of my fondest memories on Earth are of being cradled in his loving and very real, ethereal arms. If you will recall, it was in Zachariah's arms that the body I was gifted by Cassy was taken to the mother ship where we culminated our soul exchange. He has watched over our body ever since.

The children grew up during this period of my growing awareness. With their help, I have been able to fulfill my commitment to Cassy to parent "our" children. I am proud to say both Tracy and Jeff are free thinkers. They have chosen not to be trapped into status quo and the smallness of others' expectations. Like all children, their growing up included pain and disappointment, and they've had to search for themselves. Like everyone here, this is their constant path of travel — defining and re-defining themselves.

TRACY

"Mom," she said,
"I've been having these dreams lately.
People are saying the incest was my fault,
        that I'm a bad person.
I've been dreaming, too, about what happened
        . . . and, it's so real I can even smell
            his cigarettes."

I cradled her pubescent body in my arms
I told her she was special,
        that she was in no way to blame,
                and that we all loved her.
And I thought,
        I will love away the pain and confusion.

The next day we talked.
Her eyes were red and swollen,
filled with sorrow and tears,
 . . . grieving the passing of the years
        when cabbage patch dolls and Sesame
                Street occupied her mind and
                        closed out the memories.

I looked into her eyes,
     and I thought
          . . . tomorrow they will be clear
          . . . tomorrow she will be back.

She told me the next day that she didn't feel well,
     she was tired and needed to sleep.

As she turned away to go to her room,
     I thought her eyes looked glazed
          . . . more like she danced last night with the
               spirits of beer and drugs than
                    the characters of Jane Eyre
                      she had gone to the
                        library to meet.
And I thought,
     if she rests
          . . . tomorrow her eyes will be clear
          . . . tomorrow her she will be back.

"I'm not doing well," I said to myself
     as I looked across the car at her.
"What can I do to help you, Tracy,
     to lighten your load,
          so you will stop thinking about
             killing yourself?"

"I don't know,
    I don't know,"
        was her response.
And I believed her
    because here eyes were so full of longing.

I would have given my own life gladly
    to have gotten an answer
        I could put in my head
            . . . to analyze
            . . . to pray about
            . . . to formulate a plan.

And so, we both felt hopeless.

Yet, in my soul, I knew I couldn't,
    I wouldn't
        give up.

Despite the fog in both our heads,
    I was determined that
            . . . tomorrow her eyes would be clear
            . . . tomorrow she would be back.

Janis Abriel

I learned through my years of not giving up that incest is a demon battled on multiple levels. First, the physical: the unwelcome and manipulated invasion of our beautiful, gifted body—the vehicle that is necessary to our being here and experiencing the people and situations we create to get to know ourselves. Second, the chambers of our mind: our psyche is forced to deal with the unacceptable and listen to the words of an intolerant society. Third, our life force: this master of our well-being is dishonored by the entry of a negative alien energy into its very essence, its creator-self.

I also learned that incest isn't usually swept under the carpet to protect the perpetrator — it's done to protect the abused from a society that views these bodies as "damaged goods" and its owners as victims. As social victims, society's attitude forces on them a need to feel different, lesser, guilty, and mournful. "Victims" spend an inordinate amount of time trying to hide and heal or deny their experience.

Tracy and I spent years dealing with all of the above — she through drugs, alcohol, suicide attempts, and depression, and me with all the energy, money, and time I had. Ultimately, it was in our search for an answer to our pain that we were forced to look beyond society's LITTLE PICTURE and search for our answers in the spiritual realms. It was here that we stumbled into greater awareness of the BIG PICTURE, particularly the part we play as creators of our own destiny.

Zachary shared the following thought with me one day along the path of my search for peace of mind to our quandary:

Life is an illusion:

It is like hopscotch — we can skip some spaces and land on others, both intentionally. Sometimes we even do so inadvertently. Regardless, we have the skills to maneuver our way around the predicaments into which we land.

A lot of those skills are considered hidden. We don't even know what they are or where they come from. They are part of our being, our essence, but we are not necessarily acquainted with them. They are there to drive us and to help us realize our potential. They are connected to our success.

Realize these forces through prayer. Prayer is internal. It comes from our core, or should. Meditation is a trip into magical realms not limited to oneself. Use them together. The results are magical. Go and do — meditate and pray.

Zachary

And so I did — meditate and pray. Tracy and I even did it together. And through our hard work and not giving up on each other, we finally realized that Tracy wasn't a victim at all. She used this time of suffering to develop her spiritual resources and learn to be not-a-victim. Through this awareness, she knows that she co-created this experience to define herself for herself. That awareness is what it's all about! Her goal is now to assist others in overcoming social and emotional obstacles. I couldn't be prouder.

I would like to dedicate this chapter to the man who captured Cassy's heart with his genius, imagination, and affinity to animals and wilderness:

. . . the man who was Cassy's husband and her children's stepfather

. . . the man who introduced her to the phenomenon of domestic violence

. . . the man who sexually molested her daughter when she was seven years old

. . . the man who could not flee "the incest monster" in his head

. . . the man who chose to put a gun to his head to kill that monster and sacrificed his life in the process

. . . the man who gave me these memories and forced me to search to discover THERE ARE NO VICTIMS.

CHANNELING

Being A Victim Is Overrated

Q. What is the reality of this feeling we have in the third dimension that we are victims of people and circumstances?

First of all, there are no such things as people and circumstances. There are other LIFE FORCES and EXPERIENCES. These are all at your beck and call. You write the play. You choose the players. You choose the scenario. There is only OPPORTUNITY around you.

You call this thing "being a victim" because in the third dimension you feel isolated from one another. There has, particularly in the latter years of this time frame, come about a loss of what you used to have in terms of family connections. No longer do your families grow up and stay together or play together. Family members now go their own separate ways.

You have become an impersonal society in many ways, particularly in your Western civilization. Other civilizations that are not so impersonal don't have the sense of isolation from family that you do. But they might suffer isolation in terms of the political regimes that they live under. At any rate, what is transpiring upon the Earth at this particular time in response to this isolation is a resistance and an anger towards other people.

If you don't like this isolation, change it. Go out and re-develop the bonds that you want to have. You don't have to accept things as they are. It understates the ability of human civilization when you are willing to accept so readily what exists . . . instead of reaching out for What Really Is.

Let go of thinking that you must accept the status quo. If it isn't the way you like it, you have every opportunity to change it. In your civilization, you can literally change the society. In some civilizations, because of the political regimes, they cannot. But they can change the status quo in their hearts . . . they can change it in their minds . . . they can change it in small group settings.

It's time to remember that you're part of a whole, that you are a collective. Each one of you is a creator in and of yourself. You are also a collective of creators. Your affiliation, one creator with another, can raise your vibrations, your knowledge and your understanding. This will allow you to step foot off of the Earth and out into the Universe . . . out into What Really Is.

Don't feel sorry for yourselves. It is a curse of humanity that you give into feeling sorry for yourselves. You needn't accept the unacceptable, and you're not expected to. You have every opportunity to ask us questions and to ask for our assistance. Then watch for where we place the answers. They might be words from our mouths. If they're not words from our mouths, you will see the answers in the hearts of other people, in the news of everything that goes on day-to-day, in the activities and the groups that you belong to — whether it be PTA, this [spiritual development] group, the people at work, or the literature that you read.

Be creative. It is your own mind that traps you into believing that you are a victim. Break through that barrier with creativity. Look at things you've never looked at before, and there needn't ever be a reason for you to believe you're a victim again.

Q. Where did this concept of "being a victim" have its beginning?

In your species, it had its beginning when those progenitors of yours, which you call Adam and Eve, literally chose to leave what you call the Garden of Eden. The Garden of Eden was actually another dimension of consciousness in which their existence was one that was maintained for them. They chose to leave that existence because they didn't have the opportunity to make DECISIONS. Without the opportunity to make decisions, they could not be on a path of consciousness. So, they chose to bargain with their "gods." They chose to give up the luxury of no-decision-making to go into a dimension in which they had the LUXURY OF CHALLENGE.

There came to be — not in Adam and Eve's minds, because they're the ones who made the decision — but in the minds of their offspring, there developed an attitude of "Why did mom and dad blow that situation? This is doggone hard." In fact, human existence was intended to be that way. This is the way of the Universe — there are stepping stones into eternity. And this is one of them.

Q. What can we do to get beyond the "victim" mentality?

UNDERSTAND WHO YOU ARE. Know that you are literally the peer of The Creator — every second of every day you are changing every molecule and atom in your body. You may even wake up one morning, if it so be your choice, looking completely different than you did twenty-four hours before. That is the power of creation you have within you. KNOWING THIS, YOU MUST KNOW THAT YOU CANNOT BE A VICTIM.

Q. Is there anything else that would be appropriate for us to know about this subject of victimization?

This not-being-a-victim is particularly relevant to the Starseed. Their primary purpose for being on the Earth at this time is to help the Earth TRANSITION into and through the fourth dimension of consciousness. The glory of the fourth dimension is an understanding that there are no victims and being able to live accordingly. You can have that understanding this very minute. That understanding is one of the greatest gifts you can give to those you work with, you study with, you play with, you live with, you make love with.

(NOTE: Starseed are life forces who come from other planets, star systems, galaxies, and even other universes with a specific mission to help the Earth and its human inhabitants. Starseed are either born into human bodies or enter a human body "midstream" in the body's incarnation through a soul exchange.)

Q. *I want to ask about a home we had that was robbed. Everything we had was stolen. You told me that I manifested this robbery and theft. I still don't understand what you mean because I wouldn't have hurt myself like that. If it's a situation of needing to learn to move on, I can learn to move on . . . but not at a loss of what was very meaningful to me in my life.*

There are two levels of "meaningful." There is a level of

meaningful in your Earth existence that brings particular joy to your corporeal existence because there's security, there's comfort, there's a sense of belongingness that pleases very, very much.

There is also a level of meaningful connected with the life force that says, "This is not your reality. You're not really here just to be comfortable. You're not really here just to enjoy things." It's O.K. in the process if you do. But be prepared. You're never going to stand still. We, the Creators, are always keeping ourselves in transition, always moving. You will never allow yourself to stand still. So, it was the choice of your life force to manifest this robbery to keep you moving. The words of your question were filled with anger . . .

You're very right.

If you want to be angry, you have to be angry with that greater part of yourself that knew better — that knew you were too comfortable to want to change. Something had to happen, and it had to be a stick of dynamite to get you to move on.

You are in the company of many blessed entities who have experienced much of the same. They have also lost much because they were so tenacious at hanging on to where they were. They were also resistant to change and creation.

We grieve also for your loss; but we grieve mostly for the loss of your understanding that THIS IS AS IT WAS MEANT TO BE — because this is as you CHOSE it to be. A part of you that is nobler chose to manifest this experience — a part of you that is so noble it knows that its happiness does not rest in the material things of the Earth. That creator part of you knew that you had the right to experience real joy — not just satisfaction, not just comfort, not just security — but real joy. That joy went beyond the things that you had and the things that you owned.

Let go of the anger. In order to experience the joy, you have to let go of the anger. When you *do*, you'll find WHAT REALLY IS IMPORTANT. There is absolutely nothing wrong in enjoying the things of the Earth. But there is something nobler. Your spirit chose the noble road.

Zachary, Sananda, & Ezekiel

JEFF

So sensitive and strong,
        integrity firmly in tune with his life force.

The one who often went without my time,
        money, and energy so his sister
                could be maintained by it.

The one who started working when he was
        fourteen years old to live his dream.

The one who, in so many ways, had to raise
        himself because I was so involved
                . . . with work
                . . . and school
                . . . and growing into my humanness
                . . . and being about my mission.

The independent latch-key child
        who formed himself into a magnificent
                Peaceful Warrior.

Now the man I can look up to.

Janis Abriel

Jeff was a very special gift to both Cassy and I right from both of our beginnings with him.

Cassy left with me her memory of a day just weeks before Jeff's birth. She and two-year-old Tracy were on their knees praying in the nursery that had been prepared for his arrival. During the prayer Cassy looked up and saw Jeff's bright and shining life force standing near the doorway. They made an empathic connection that she recognized immediately the day his tiny five-pound body was put in her arms. She knew the first time she gazed into his eyes that an eternal bond between them was already in place. He was her gift from the Universe.

That loving bond created a treasure box full of fond memories . . . memories and beautiful feelings I inherited of their times together making bunny rabbit pancakes, hunting for frogs, setting off fire works, playing at the park, visiting the zoo, raising pet lizards and turtles, searching for an escaped snake, visiting the pet shop to cheer up a glum day.

However, one memory stands out above all the others in my mind. When Jeff was four, he and Cassy were watching a television show about a man whose house was burned down in a violent act of bigotry. The man had worked very hard to buy the land and materials for erecting the house. He built it with his own hands. With a maturity far beyond his four years, Jeff leaned over to Cassy and said, "They shouldn't have done that, mommy. That was HIS house. They were being mean." By four, Jeff already had a strong sense of justice.

These memories, and many more, forged a bond

between Cassy and Jeff that prevailed through divorce, domestic violence, and the first day of kindergarten. Their love for each other and their communal lessons are no doubt what helped make Jeff the remarkable ten year old boy who inherited me.

Right from my inception, Jeff's gentle spirit nurtured me into my humanness. In return, I helped him with his homework and introduced him to the Universe. He was really my superior, however. He taught me many lessons. One of the first was the principle of integrity.

When Jeff was only eleven years old, his best friend started smoking and stealing from the corner convenience store with their other friends. Jeff didn't give into peer pressure. Instead, he detached from his friends. It tore at my heart strings to see him walk to school by himself, the pain of loneliness flickering in his eyes.

It didn't take long, however, for a brighter light to ignite in those beautiful brown eyes — one that comes from honoring the values he had built for himself. In the process, personal strength and self-esteem became even more apparent than the inches he was adding to his stature.

About a year later Jeff came up against some school bullies. He spoke his mind and got his head smashed into a locker. I enrolled him in karate classes so he could learn to defend himself. In the process, he developed self-confidence and another value — violence has no value. He has staunchly walked the way of the peaceful warrior ever since.

Jeff was only twelve when Tracy fell into her deep

depression over the incest. Despite his tender age, when I told him that I needed his support to help both Tracy and I through this very rough time, he never wavered. He became my rock. He had to go without many things his friends had, but he never complained, not even once. He taught me trust and confidence.

Jeff and I manifested some other tough lessons in living before he grew up and set out on his own. But together we mustered the strength from spiritual resources to keep working our way up third dimensional mountains. Now that Jeff is an adult, he's working on those mountains mostly by himself. I would like to think that what we employed to get us through the challenges we encountered and conquered together will see him standing on many mountaintops.

What worked for us was LOVE.

CHANNELING

Spiritual Solutions to Material Problems

Q. What purpose do problems serve in our lives here on Earth?

To teach you what YOU want to know. You create your problems to challenge yourselves to greater heights.

Q. You may have just answered this, but is there a root cause common to all problems we experience here in the third dimensional Earth consciousness?

Yes, there is. The desire to experience JOY is the root cause of all of your problems. Integral to that desire is your need to grow in consciousness. Though you do not recognize this on a conscious level, on your supraconscious level you do know this.

Q. Why do some people experience more crisis or problems in their lives than other people?

There isn't one answer to that question. There are a multiple number of answers. Some people manifest extraordinary crisis and problems in their lives because they choose to learn a great deal in this existence. It may be that their consciousness is very high, but they're pushing themselves to greater heights. Or, they may be on a lesser level of consciousness pushing themselves to greater heights. They want to know. IT'S A THIRST TO KNOW.

Q. Why do some people find it more difficult to solve problems than others?

Those who have more difficulty solving problems are the people who have either sunk their teeth into the material, or they have bought into the structure of organizations that choose to control them. In either case, they feel disempowered. They don't know their own power because they're looking outside of themselves to leaders of this, to leaders of that, a savior for this, a savior for that. They don't believe in their own power.

Q. Is there a relationship between emotions and problems?

In the area of health — physical, mental, emotional, and spiritual — the emotional dis-ease that one feels inside manifests in dis-ease externally. So, the emotional balance of the person will reflect outwardly. This conspicuous demonstration urges the person to consciously recognize the emotional dis-ease.

Q. You've talked to us before about the power of thought. Can you please describe the nature of thought for us?

Thought is everything that you are and everything that you can be. Thought is the power of creation. Was it not the thought of The Creator that created you? Now you are all that YOU THINK you are. Thought is your vehicle for movement into higher vibrations and consciousness.

Q. Is there a difference between what we call the brain and what we call the mind? If there is, would you please give us a definition of each.

The human brain is the material matter that processes the subconscious and supraconscious levels of your understanding into your CONSCIOUS awareness. The mind, also called the Universal Mind, is that area where your supraconsciousness can access extra-ordinary information and experiences — ALL THAT IS and What Really Is. It is the realm of your life force.

Q. We read a lot about affirmations. Are affirmations really as powerful as we are told they are?

Absolutely. Affirmations are a human vehicle for manifesting your thoughts. Because they are thought-centered, they have the power to create, to desecrate, to take you forward, to take you backwards, to help you experience anything that you want. So, yes, they are very powerful.

Q. We have been told that the phrase "I am" is a powerful affirmation. Are there other forms of affirmations that are preferable to use?

The phrase "I am" is powerful because it honors and respects your true being. For that reason, it is what "gets the ear" of the Universe. It is how we hear you.

We suggest that you open your affirmations with the words, "By intent." Or use the words "by intent" someplace in your affirmation. It is by your intent, your pure intent, that you open the door that gives you access into ALL THAT IS.

Q. I'm using a technique employing energy in the body to release negative thoughts from other lifetimes. Should I teach this technique to people who have never worked with this kind of energy?

It is very important for people to be able to release negative thoughts and feelings. Unfortunately, it is a technique that has been lost over time. Did you know that in past times people knew how to do this very effectively but lost that ability? They became so involved with other things — fighting, violence, trying to learn more than the other person, trying to build a greater house, trying to have the nicer things — that they forgot how to release.

Past lives can have a great deal to do with what's going on in the present existence of a person, depending upon what the person is doing in this existence. It is very helpful to release negative thoughts from these past lives, just as it is appropriate to release negativity from the subconscious in the present existence. So, if you use energy-release techniques that you are finding effective, by all means continue with that.

We don't suggest that people walk in the past a great deal. We suggest that they live in the present. So many people keep trying to jump into their past lives in order to understand their present. The very best way to understand your present existence is by growing in consciousness through LIVING IN THE PRESENT.

So, don't encourage too many people to dig into their past lives unless you find that there is a significant connection with the present. Usually you can find one or two, perhaps three lifetimes that impinge upon the present lifetime. Do it, deal with it, get rid of the negativity, and encourage your people to live in the present and develop their consciousness.

Zachary, Sananda, & Ezekiel

OF MEN & ANGELS

I spent the summer of 1990 with Tamara, mostly under a tree in the park. I found out then that transcendent beings come and go in our lives depending on their purpose for being with us.

Tamara whispered her name in my ear one morning on my way to work. I didn't understand. So, she continued to pop in and out of my auditory senses until I figured out she had been sent to serve as my guide. And guide me, she did!

I looked forward anxiously to our get-togethers in the park. Armed with pen and paper, I headed down the hill on my bike every weekend, anticipating capturing the words of wisdom she shared with me under our tree. Her words inspired me to greater understanding of existence . . . my existence . . . our existence. They cast a spell over my life. They empowered me to embark on a journey to fulfill one of Cassy's dreams.

That summer, I left corporate America and started college to complete Cassy's Bachelor's degree in Communications and Journalism. The Universe dropped the perfect job for accomplishing this in my lap. The rest of the necessary arrangements fell into place like honey in a jar. I knew I was headed in the right direction because synchronicity is a highly visible affirmation. I graduated in 1992. The diploma has Cassy's name on it. I was honored to do this for her.

That fall, I started a Master's program I had designed in Interdisciplinary Studies. Tamara had moved on and out of my life almost two years earlier. Though I had been more than busy with classes, study, research, work, and raising two children, her absence was a deeply felt loss in my life. Our time together had been little more than six months, yet I missed her wisdom and vitality beyond words. I experienced a new kind of loneliness in her absence and wondered if I would ever again experience a relationship with another transcendent being.

The answer to that question came in the spring of 1993. Zachary knocked on the door of my conscious senses. I heard his voice and saw the visions he placed in my mind. His first words to me were an announcement that he had come "on board." I had experienced enough comings-and-goings of Transcendents, so I invited Zachary to stay on board only if he wasn't going to abandon ship.

Affirmative! He committed to a life-time contract. We began a relationship that changed my reality forever. He became my best friend, my mentor, my guide into the Universe. He became MY Transcendent!

All the questions Cassy and I had accumulated over the last forty-four years became the fodder that nourished my soul to a point of exaltation at this time. Worlds of knowledge were at my disposal, and they played out like videos in my mind providing me with answers to all of those questions. I asked questions about the purpose of life, religion, spirituality, angels, prayer, the Bible, animals, and extraterrestrials. In retrospect, my questions were pretty unsophisticated. Eventually, I even ran out of unsophisticated questions.

That didn't prove to be an obstacle to Zachary. He continued on with my education, despite me. He just kept giving me answers without my asking any questions . . . and those no-questions were a lot better than the ones I had been asking. That got me to thinking . . . thinking a lot deeper than I ever had. Pretty soon I realized that I was only getting half the picture. I needed more insight into the flip side of the "existence coin." I became obsessed with a desire to visit the other side of life. I wanted to visit "death."

In lieu of dying, I opted for a NEAR death experience to round out my understanding of existence. I submitted my request for a near death experience to Zachary . . . and sat back and waited for his response.

I can only hope Zachary didn't double over laughing at my request like my friend Evlyn did. When she recovered her composure, Evlyn assured me that there were other ways of getting the information I wanted. She was right.

Two weeks later my Uncle Dick died. I didn't even have time to deal with the loss before he started whispering in my ear. He was now a citizen of the ethereal realm. Because life forces don't have the same limitations as human bodies, he could communicate with me much like Zachary did . . . on the back of higher vibrations. Using my ability to visit the ethereal realms, Dick and I were able to walk and talk together in the land of the spirit.

Dick showed me a place of no-fear and we laughed in

the light of higher vibrations. He taught me about the process, nature, and purpose of death. He showed me that on the other side of life there is no judgment. He told me the story of Gaia, the dynamic entity upon whose back we walk, known here as the Earth. He showed me the reality of energy, the feelings behind vibrations, and the freedom of positive thinking. He introduced me to a reality I would visit often in the coming years.

My memories of Uncle Dick were filled with his wonderful sense of humor and endearing charm. Because he had lived a long, fulfilling life and his death experience was peaceful, those qualities radiated immediately in his channelings to me. They also assisted in his swift adjustment to the ethereal realms. Since then, my walks in the world of the disincarnated have taught me that the length and difficulty of one's transition into this world are in part dependent on the circumstances of death.

Dick joined forces with Zachary in my spiritual education. This time brought great peace to me — a "peace beyond all understanding." Nurtured and guided by Zachary and Dick, the next eighteen months brought crystal-clear meaning to the concept of divine order. I had come home. Zachary and Dick had opened a doorway into another reality for me. When I stepped over that threshold, I remembered What Really Is. During those eighteen months, I created my reality. Literally everything I wished for manifested, as it does in the higher dimensions of consciousness.

The experiences of this time etched deep in my heart the

connection we each have with THE WHOLE. We are all part of one another. We are not only companions of the Transcendents, WE ARE THE TRANSCENDENTS in human form. It is only our lack of self-knowing and our negative thinking that keeps us from remembering that! We need only use our CREATIVITY to step beyond the status quo if we want to remember.

   ... And, when we do remember, our greatest realization will be that we are all creators ... creators of our own realities ... cut from the same ethereal cloth as The Creator.

"YOU ARE MY FOOTSTEPS"

The Creator

CHANNELING

Creation & the Purpose of Existence

Dearly Beloved Transcendents,

We have come to speak to you about that subject which is at the crux of human existence — creation and the PURPOSE of human existence. In the third dimensional Earth realm, we tend to look at the LITTLE PICTURE — Earth existence only. We would like to ask you some questions tonight about the BIG PICTURE — the Universe and our part in it. We would also like to invite The Creator to participate in our discussion if (S)he so chooses.

JAN: The Creator is here with us tonight. (S)he is very pleased with our topic and appreciates the invitation to participate with us. The Creator is not a persona, but a presence. I am surrounded with this presence. It is so overwhelming, strong, forceful, and powerful. I just feel enveloped in it. It is incredible! What a blessing.

Q. *Can you tell us HOW we were created? Is the "Big Bang" theory correct?*

The push and tug and the pull of it all — how applicable that you should meet on this night of the full moon when you experience the pull of the magnetic waves. For herein is your creation. Herein is your existence. You are the magnetic waves, and the energy, and the vibrations of everything that exists, ever existed, and ever will exist.

You are that part of me that was my heart and my soul, and I wanted to share existence with you in the grandest way, in the grandest scheme of things . . . the experience of differences . . . the experience of so many opportunities . . . the experience of so many insights, foresights, and putting-it-togetherness.

So, I chose to allow us all — me, The Creator . . . you, the creators . . . we, all one creator — to experience and create the grandest potential. And I sent out my heart and my soul — YOU — in many different forms, on many roads, and in many directions to EXPERIENCE.

So, you are my FOOTSTEPS. And even though our footsteps go in many different directions, at some point we always come back together in the real realms to discuss our experiences and our learnings.

Therefore, to some extent, what you call your "Big Bang"

theory is appropriate. In essence, it was a peaceful severing. It was a peaceful maneuver into many different footsteps.

In each one of all of us there is totality, and beauty, and the grandest of the grandest. We are all ONE. I want you to remember that. Even though we look different, even though we walk different paths, even though we have different values, we are all ONE.

You are here to experience, and there is no one experience grander than another. Each experience is noble, even if it does not appear to be. Each experience is noble and worthy because it feeds ALL of us understanding and greater comprehension of who we all are as ONE. We are defining that word you call "ONE" with every step we take.

Q. Were all of our Universe and its inhabitants created at the same time?

Indeed, they were; although existence has been a *process*. THE PLAN was formulated at one time, and through The Plan much has evolved. So, the thought of it all began at the same time. The actual becoming in some cases was evolutionary, but the concept was all at the beginning.

Q. How can the concept of "beginning" be explained? Didn't existence have to begin somewhere? But how can something begin out of nothing?

Perhaps you could forget that the words "begin" and "nothing" have meaning. You created those words to help your understanding. In fact, there is no beginning. There is no end. There is nothing. There is only everything in totality as it exists in the NOW.

It is difficult for you to understand this in your third dimensional consciousness. If you choose to understand, ask me and the understanding will come into your heart and intuition — though the words will not be in your grasp. Just remember, THE CREATION IS NOW.

Q. What is our intended relationship to the rest of the Universe and it's inhabitants?

To assist each other in experiences. To assist each other in attaining nobility in these experiences — by refining your vibrations through the shaggiest of vibrations, through the harshest of vibrations, through the most horrendous of experiences — so that we might all again blend together in uniqueness and oneness.

Q. Is there more than one Universe? Does each Universe have a different Creator?

There are many Universes. There is so much more beyond your comprehension. I wish that you could even get a glimpse of it. If you were able to get a glimpse of it, you would understand your grandness. You would understand your purpose. You would understand your potential. You would understand that concept called unconditional love.

Indeed, there are multitudes of worlds and Universes. There are multitudes of entities, beliefs, philosophies, credentials, learnings, yearnings, knowings, and not-knowings. And we created all of this together . . . you and I.

Our creator-feet take us to every corner of every Universe and allow us to experience all that we can imagine and all that we can create with our imagination. For you, my little footsteps, are also my eyes, my ears, my heart, myself. To each and every one of you, I owe what I am.

Q. *WHY were we all created?*

We just talked about the purpose of The Creation. To summarize that — to experience the opportunity of creating everything we can potentially create . . . to understand that we can create beyond our own belief, beyond our knowledge, beyond our own potential . . . to grow with one another, to serve one another, to love one another . . . to ultimately refine our vibrations into a unity of the highest concept of consciousness . . . then, to understand there are no boundaries, there are no limitations, there is only opportunity for creation in everything that we do, and think, and feel.

Q. *We are told that we will someday rejoin The Creator and become that ONE entity again, as it was before our creation. If that is so, will not our uniqueness as multiplicities of individuals be lost? It would seem to be a boring existence. Is this "the end" of existence?*

There is no end of existence, as you would think of it. THERE IS ONLY MORE.

Will uniqueness be lost? No. In that perfect refinement will exist the most beautiful uniqueness that could ever be imagined. There is a sea of uniqueness that resonates throughout the Universe, and it is the glory of the Universe that such uniqueness exists in its finest form. When we have refined our vibrations to the point where we again REMEMBER that we are all ONE, we may still be in different forms, but we will still be ONE. Uniqueness will be preserved, oneness will be remembered, and consciousness will be honored and respected for what it truly is.

Q. What is the singular most important thought that we should carry with us throughout our existence?

If there is one word that I would leave with you it would be "MORE." You make out of that what you want to. That is your challenge — MORE.

Q. What is the most appropriate name to call our Creator?

In your existence, "The Creator" is probably the most appropriate name. I have been called by many different names ... many, many different concepts. In your existence there are so many different concepts of what I am, of who I am, of what I am about, but the name that seems to best suit your understanding and the concept that THERE IS ALWAYS MORE is "The Creator." I accept this honorary title that you bestow upon me, and I give it back to you and ask you all to use the same name.

If you choose to call me The Creator because I am that wellspring from which you came, then you might want to call me SOURCE and call yourselves CREATORS.

Q. Is there a difference between The Creator and that one humans call God?

Yes and no.   That word you use, "God," is what you would refer to as The Creator — that entity who gave you what you call your beginning (which we call your NOW). However, there is much confusion and misunderstanding in your dimension as to what we all are, you and I.

If you would let go of your need to believe that some things are bad, you would have a more appropriate concept of what Creator and creation is. For everything is created in glory, the painful as well as the joyful. There is no ill-intent in any creation. Only the most positive of intent exists in any creation, even if the results might seem painful to you.

You fear that thing you call your God. In fact, there is nothing to fear in either you or I. If there is only experience to grow and to refine, there must be something jagged to refine.

But the jagged is beautiful, purposeful, and there is nothing to fear in it.

When you realize that YOU create your pain, you can let go of that all mighty, all powerful, all knowing, all punishing, all judgmental entity that you call God. For, there is no such thing. There are only CREATORS in existence, and each of you is one. Let go of your need to confine things. Let go of your need to systematize things so that they make total sense. If you would learn to accept things that don't make total sense — but have the potential for making total sense as you grow — then you would better understand this whole process. Then you could let go of that concept that you call God and understand that there are only CREATORS.

Q. How do we develop a personal relationship with our Creator?

By developing a personal relationship with yourself and with others around you — thereby learning who you are. When you understand who you are, you will have a personal relationship with me. KNOW YOURSELF, KNOW ME.

Q. How does creation relate to the TRANSITION into the fourth dimensional consciousness we are going through here on Earth? Is there anything else we have forgotten to ask that would be appropriate for us as Starseed to know at this time? Is there anything that would be appropriate for us to share with our other brothers and sisters upon the Earth?

The concept, THERE IS ALWAYS MORE, is what you should be sharing with your brothers and sisters upon the Earth. That is to answer your last question first.

What is this thing that you are going through now? What is this thing that you call a TRANSITION? It is part of what we have all created on our path to refining vibrations, to understanding the sea of uniqueness that is our existence.

There is one sea, and in that sea there are many drops of water. Each drop of water is unique, and each drop is necessary to make up the sea of wholeness, of oneness. This thing that you go through, this thing that you call a TRANSITION into the next dimension, is a ripple in the sea . . . a ripple that is necessary to bring the sea to greater smoothness.

Just as the waves refine, break down, and smooth out the rocks upon the shore, so also does this TRANSITION smooth out the vibrations. Thereby, it brings you into a space of GREATER UNDERSTANDING. It pulls you deeper into the midst of the sea — further into all of the other drops of the sea — so you can understand where the other drops came from, what they have done, and what part they constitute in the sea.

Likewise, as you go into this other dimension, you will gain greater understanding of what creation and existence is all about. You will have greater access to the understanding of the experiences of those who exist beyond you that you have not known heretofore. For as you experience this TRANSITION, you will see me.

You will also meet your brothers and sisters in the sky. You will become privy to the experiences that they have had and what they have learned from their experiences. You will experience yourself in their thoughts, their feelings, their emotions, their beliefs, and their philosophies. You will become more integrated into the sea, and their uniqueness will become a gift to you as you all blend in this huge, huge sea of diversity.

Through this smoothing of the sea, you will be able to pull this greater understanding of creation and existence into you by the power of your thought. You will be able to feel the experiences of all of these other beautiful entities you have heretofore not been able to experience. This is part of your creation — to experience more. And there will be even more beyond this. But this is a beautiful step in your experiencing more of creation.

Q. What is the photon belt that we are hearing so much about? Is it going to change the Earth from the third dimension to the fourth dimension?

It is simply a different kind of vibration and energy. It is a mass of energy. Your whole solar system is moving into this nebula of energy. You have passed through it before and you are ready to pass through it again.

The photon energy is different than the energy you are used to. Because of this, the vibrations in your body are going to change. It is intended, and part of the plan that you created, that this would take you into a greater understanding of existence.

Q. Could you recommend a simple exercise that would help us on the Earth plane to regain our memories of past lifetimes and our full abilities as spiritual beings?

There is no such thing as a simple exercise for doing this. That is what EXPERIENCE is all about. It is digging your hand into the Earth and working it.

How do you regain you remembrance? You regain your remembrance by getting out there and experiencing MORE. Then use the power of the CREATOR within you — that thing that you call your life force — to understand more fully. You can even access the understanding of other people to help in your own understanding.

There is no simple way. There is only doing, exper-iencing, and discerning. Don't allow others to tell you that you are limited, that you are wrong, that you can't do what you want to do. Break through those barriers. Understand that you have no limitations. When you firmly believe this, you can manifest your spiritual being in its fullness.

Q. What is the best thing that we can do to accelerate the planet Earth to a more spiritual realm?

That is a very good question. You can do this by accelerating your OWN spiritual growth and then doing something with it. It does no good to accelerate your own consciousness and then hide it under a bushel basket. You are here to help others. So, when you learn something, you are to talk to other people about it.

I hear so many people upon your Earth trying to negate that SHARING by calling it bragging, pushing, or forcing. So, share your understanding with love. Offer it and don't force it. You can put it into words that go into books, lectures, or workshops. Or you can simply share it with other individuals — not by forcing — because you will never, never help planet Earth nor the inhabitants of the Earth by forcing anything upon them.

Beloved Creator, we want to thank you for being here with us this evening. We are honored to have been able to speak with you and enjoy your wisdom.

I wish to express my thanks to you and let you know how

much your footsteps and existence have meant to me. We are all one. We are all beloved. We are all creators. Some day we will all stand face-to-face . . . and we will recognize our uniqueness, our oneness, and the power we manifest together. Thank you.

The Creator

RELATIONSHIPS & SPIRITUALITY

I have learned, since my arrival on Earth, that spirituality in the third dimensional Earth plane comes in steps and evolves primarily through experiences provided in relationships. The Creator gave us our very first example of this universal truth.

From The Creator's own explanation earlier in this book, we learned that before we existed, (s)he existed as a complete, self-contained being of pure energy in "solitary confinement." This made for a lot of peace and stability, but it certainly didn't allow for much excitement . . . and dynamic growth was virtually non-existent. The Creator wanted more.

So at some point in existence, The Creator severed into billions and billions of energetic life forces — YOU — forever changing the course of existence.

All of these life forces also became creators. Each of these creators had ALL of the characteristics of The Source Creator . . . and something more. Now in numbers, these co-creators (as I have come to call them) could interact with one another. This interaction allowed them to do more than just think about existence. They could EXPERIENCE existence.

Through the phenomenon of experience, the Universe became a dynamic, vital birthing place for activity. Activity gave birth to consciousness. Consciousness gave birth to joy.

And through cosmic DNA, The Creator could now share the joy the co-creators manifested for themselves through their growth in consciousness.

So it is that relationships and spirituality became inextricably intertwined.

From the heart of The Creator
sprang strong spiritual purpose,
nurturing, and a commitment to peacemaking.

The Creator called this energy "female"
and placed female next to male on a battlefield.

"Male and female," said The Creator,
"you are here to challenge each other
. . . so that female will learn to call up her strength
and male will recall his softness."

"Only when you have combined and balanced
strength & softness
will you be allowed to leave the battlefield."

Zachary

I have witnessed some people who appear to be very "lucky" in having comparatively happy relationships. I have seen others who seem to be "plagued" with one or a series of joyless relationships. "Why is this?," I wondered.

In response to my inquiry, the Transcendents taught me the Principle of Creation. I learned that we actively CHOOSE the nature of our relationships. "What!," you say. "I would never choose to be in a miserable relationship." And, you're right — CONSCIOUSLY you wouldn't do such a thing. However, on your SUPRA-CONSCIOUS level, you have greater insight.

On this supra-conscious level you choose relationships that will provide you with the experiences you need to grow in greater understanding of yourself and the ways of the Universe. This could mean challenges, and even (ouch) pain.

How your spirituality grows through your conscious experience is up to you. You will bring your own unique personality and insight to each experience. If you follow through and integrate the experience successfully into your consciousness, that integration will include these three steps. You can call it WILL, free will.

1. Wonderment
2. Intellect
3. Living the Lesson

Briefly, this means that you first make spirituality a conscious goal. This choice to make spirituality your goal oftentimes has its beginning in an experience that opens you up to a belief in a BIGGER PICTURE — a picture that inspires a sense of awe or WONDERMENT in existence. Then your spiritual goal *takes form* when you integrate principles of higher consciousness into your INTELLECT. Finally, your spiritual goal *comes to life* when you move past your intellect and into LIVING those ways of higher consciousness. To show you how this works, I will give you an example from my own life.

When I came here, I inherited Cassy's memories. The memories I inherited of her relationship with Collin included physical and verbal abuse, deceit, and infidelity. These memories were the product of my brain. I experienced them as pictures and words, similar to watching a movie about domestic violence . . . but, from a distance. I didn't FEEL any personal connection with their drama . . . because I had never experienced them in the heart of my OWN life force.

Six months after my soul exchange with Cassy, I began a relationship with a man I came to understand was intended to be my life mate. By the time I met him, I had already identified spirituality as my primary goal in this existence. My cosmic memory was of that BIGGER PICTURE, and my walks and talks in other dimensions were a matter of awe and WONDERMENT (step 1).

This relationship started out wonderfully and was supportive to my spiritual goals. Five months later something unexpected showed up — a need in my companion to control my life, right down to the smallest details. Cassy was independent. So was I. So, memories and my own personal characteristics resisted. This angered him and he responded with verbal abuse. Within a few weeks he grabbed me by the throat and threw me up against a bathroom wall. I felt angry and disgusted. That was enough dishonor for me. I left immediately.

This man called me a few months later and asked if he could talk to me. I picked a place in a public setting where we could have lunch. We talked briefly and he indicated he wanted to explore renovating the relationship. He asked if he could help me with a move I was making in a few days. I told him that probably wasn't practical, as I only had time to pack and not to talk. He assured me that was all right with him. However, he showed up wanting to talk. When I told him I couldn't, he became furious. He backed me into a room and his mouth opened like a trash can spewing garbage.

I walked around for many months feeling the weight and smelling the stench of that garbage. I couldn't shake the picture of his face — jaws clenched, eyes blazing, and the dark, heavy energy surrounding him, like waste churning in the heat and darkness of a dumpster.

I knew from Cassy's memories that relationships without honor and respect are low on the consciousness totem pole. They can serve a purpose, but we must move our way up the totem pole to find peace, satisfaction, and joy. Moving up that totem pole requires change and effort.

I also learned from Cassy that if abusers deny their actions, there will be no end to the abuse. At that point, the other partner can only re-empower himself or herself by taking steps to ensure that he or she is treated with respect thereafter. My intended life mate was in denial of his behavior. The dishonor was bound to continue, but I determined the relationship wouldn't.

Cassy's memories also held visions of a society largely in denial of relationship abuse — a collective consciousness that found it easier to sweep this abortion of consciousness under a rug than to DO something about it. Later when I was working for the court system as a professional mediator, I learned that the court system often leans towards protecting the "integrity" of the perpetrator rather than the life and respect of the abused.

When society does respond to someone being physically abused, there must be dramatic, unquestionable, visual proof of the damage and dishonor. This is low on the consciousness totem pole. But there's one totem lower on the pole that signifies the poorest state of a society's group consciousness. That is denying the damage and dishonor of VERBAL abuse . . . because it is FELT and NOT SEEN.

Verbal abuse can be as destructive as physical abuse — sometimes more destructive — because it is an affront to our immortal life force. I can assure you this is so because I experienced it. Verbal abuse gives birth to low self-esteem and anger. It is an instigator of fear, dishonesty, and violence.

Our life force knows itself as being of the stuff of The Creator, deserving to be treated only with honor and respect. Verbal abuse tries to deny that *Creator-connection*. That is a crime of cosmic proportions.

My INTELLECT absorbed the principles I had learned from this experience (step 2), and I was ready to move on. It helped me to draw on the old adage, "The best revenge is a life well lived." So, I made a commitment to myself to LIVE the lesson I had learned from this relationship. I decided to bring life to the concepts of HONOR and RESPECT by helping people remember and understand their *Creator-connection* (step 3).

My intent is that this book reach thousands, even millions, of other beautiful life forces like yourself and remind you of how special you are . . . and that nobody can ever take that away from you . . . not even yourself.

After having dedicated myself to the concepts of honor and respect, I came up against a wall I didn't know how to surmount. Deep in contemplation one day, I determined that there had been either a major mistake in the creation process or the human species was the brunt of a distorted joke. Somehow men and women had been created with, what seemed to me to be, too many irreconcilable differences to allow for honor and respect.

As I was stewing over this quandary, Zachary shared the following insights with me. I've found these insights to be very helpful in understanding the importance of these differences in learning how to maintain BALANCE within our own individual being while living our relationships.

Q. Zachary, why are men and women so different?

To show the different sides of existence:

- No two things are alike.
- The beauty in living is in the differences, not the similarities.
- True joy and peace come with honoring differences.

But it's not working! Look at the escalating domestic abuse and spousal/companion murders.

That is because many people are going backwards — greed and power have more substance to them than What Really Is.

Q. What is "What Really Is?"

Our bare substance, our spirit, our energy — OUR LIFE FORCE.

True wealth is not in what can be seen, or touched, or pleasured. What REALLY touches us is what we cannot see or feel with hands of flesh and blood. When we get beyond the physical, men and women are very much alike.

On Earth, men are aggressive because survival dictates it. Women are more passive because they must balance the scales of existence.

Women are really very strong and, thereby, frustrated by this role. Their demanding honor in society will make it less necessary for men to show their power. Then men will be able to rest their stance and find joy in their softness.

NOW the purpose of men is to challenge women to set their souls free. Passivity on the part of women does not help either themselves or men. Men respect strength and yet set up barriers for women to keep them from attaining it. It is necessary to be challenged to grow — men challenge women so they will become strong, and women challenge men so they will recall their softness. True energy, true being, is a combination and BALANCE of both.

Relationships that do not assist each other in developing this balance are not productive. There is no shame in ending such relationships. It shows good sense and understanding, and it typifies the need of the spirit to be free to find itself.

This is done by questioning and challenging the status quo. When the human stagnates, so does the spirit. Life is meant to be joyous and exciting, not predictable and passive.

You should encourage your children to be individuals, so they will maximize their earthly existence. When humans "clump" together, the soul digresses into unseen paths of violence and aggression in an effort to be set free from the bonds of expectations.

Q. *What of monogamy?*

It has two sides, two possibilities. It can be a display of honor for another person's feelings, which bonds souls and represents a commitment to each other's individual paths. If it is done out of fear, however, it is a farce and has no value.

It is a glorious thing to have a partner committed to honoring the needs of the other partner . . . it is also rare. Most humans are very selfish. A state of disrepair has resulted — something like a run-down house that has not been maintained and afforded the respect due it as a different form of energy.

If sex is used to magnify feelings of love and respect, it gets you going in the right direction. If used aggressively, however, no one benefits. It will seem intolerable to the person suffering the aggression. His or her energy may diminish. Therein is the real violation.

However, such an experience need only be a temporary setback. The energy sacrificed to the experience can be replenished by taking command of one's thoughts and by not passing judgment.

This holds true for all experiences viewed by

human nature as negative — THE RESULT OF LOOKING AT A SLICE OF LIFE, NOT THE WHOLE THING.

Remember, the purpose of earthly existence is to understand and come to grips with your true nature — ENERGY — a glorious state of existence that includes limitless possibilities and expression.

Zachary

Relationships, for me, have been more of a classroom than the ones I've sat in for so many years. They have spawned insight, determination, and action. That is because they are real. That's not to say the three R's don't have value. They are tools for success. But relationships are more than a tool. They are participatory. And we as co-creators define the action.

I have had a number of relationships since the one I described above. I have learned something worth living from each one. Even in this relationship, I observed many things worth activating in my own life. In addition to the challenges this man posed, he exhibited great focus, responsibility, determination, and loyalty. Though he had difficulty seeing me as anything other than an extension of himself, he did understand a lot about himself. He knew what he wanted and was willing to work for it.

After I moved past this relationship, Peter and I mended fences. Peter was the man I had "inherited" from Cassy, and who had left the relationship shortly after our soul exchange. Subsequently, we became companions for many years. He was even-tempered, stable, and committed. He provided me with a wonderful sense of security. As a result, I experienced a great deal of peace in this relationship. Though we were not walking the same spiritual path, he never thwarted me and often supported me. He was and still is wonderful to my children. In addition to these qualities, he had many others worth emulating. I learned that spirituality blossoms in such fertile, nurturing soil.

Other relationships with friends, family, and co-workers, as well as romantic liaisons have taught me the value of honesty, integrity, patience, differences, generosity, positive attitudes, playfulness, kindness, and limitless thinking, among a multitude of other things. My relationship with the Transcendents has taught me literally to "aim for the sky."

All my relationships have been a lesson in living . . . a lesson worth living. I am thankful for all of them because, pain included, they have gone into the making, remembering, and understanding of ME. I've found a great deal of satisfaction in working my way up the consciousness totem pole with the help of these lessons.

CHANNELING

Taking the Hardship Out of Relationship

Q. Are relationships really NECESSARY? If so, why?

For those of you in the third dimensional Earth realm, relationships are necessary. They are necessary because you learn from one another. You see yourselves in each other's faces. You see your weaknesses and you see your strengths. Your strengths and your weaknesses are magnified by others. For this reason, you learn from them.

Once you have stepped onto the love conveyer belt, so to speak, you choose to have relationships because you want to share your love with one another. Much joy and other wonderful feelings come from sharing your love with one another.

Those of you in the third dimensional Earth realm are in a process of growth which involves experiencing positives and negatives. Those of us in the eighth dimensional realm have been in that third dimensional realm. We remember well having experienced what you call opposition. In reality it is not opposition. It is feedback — feedback of feelings. In your existence there are two feelings — love and fear. You can experience these in your relationships.

It would be easy to work out of ego were it not for other people. It is your relationships that either feed your ego or push you to work from a space of love — self-love and love of others.

Q. Do astrological signs and movements affect relationships? If so, how?

Yes, particularly for those of you in this dimension at this time. You come into existence at a certain time, at a certain place, and to certain people. Remember, life is not a craps game. You don't shoot and hope that it ends up a "winner."

You have something to say in all of this. And you say a tremendous amount of it before you even come here. You choose what it is you want to experience. You choose what it is you want to learn and how you want to raise your vibrations.

The ebb and flow of the electromagnetic waves of the solar system — those things that you push into the realm of astrology — are all very important in assuring that you have those OPPORTUNITIES you chose before you come here . . . and those you choose while you are here. You are creating constantly, before and during this process you call living.

Astrological links affect you through electromagnetic waves. This is because you are ENERGY and EVERYTHING in your existence, though you do not see it as that, is energy. So, the ebb and the flow, the pull and the push of these electromagnetic energies give you what you call "propensities" to do life a certain way. Every propensity is just an opportunity to grow and to advance. It is something that can be changed, overcome, or embraced.

Propensities provide you the opportunity for growth in conjunction with relationships. These propensities set up experiences for you to learn those things that you pre-chose and that you are choosing and creating now.

Astrological links are part of what we call the FORM OF THE UNIVERSE — which gives structure to existence. It was this FORM, which all of us created together in developing this system within our Universe, that ensures the growth of consciousness. Through this FORM, the original intent of The Creator will be fulfilled through us.

Q. What is your opinion of intimate relationships between people of the same sex?

You have created a philosophy within your system of duality that says sexual relationships must be between a man and a woman and, otherwise, are wrong. You do that to create some kind of structure in which you can ensure the continuation of your species upon the Earth. In fact, there is more to intimacy than continuation of a species.

Intimacy is a process of evolvement in consciousness. So that you are not shocked by what we say, you need to understand that for us intimacy is literally a touching of the life forces. We do not deal with the corporeal forms that you do. We have ethereal bodies.

What we do when we show appreciation for one another, when we show honor, respect, and love for one another, is that we literally walk into one another's life forces. This is similar to what you say is the "two becoming one" in a conjugal relationship. But in our world there are no taboos. We show our appreciation and our love for all entities — male energy, female energy, energy that is combined. Here we see no separation.

You have made intimacy a moral issue. Intimacy in the BIG PICTURE, as you call it, is not a moral issue. Intimacy is just intimacy. It is APPRECIATION for one another.

In your third dimensional world, you have attached rules to intimacy — rights, obligations, good, and evil. You have done that because it gives you a feeling of structure. But you can step beyond that structure and see that intimacy is just appreciation. Then there is no judgment when intimacy is between a male energy and a male energy or a female energy and a female energy who just happen to have corporeal bodies between them.

Try to step out of your LITTLE PICTURE. Try to step out of the rules and regulations that you have created and grow in consciousness. Grow to greater knowledge and understanding. Grow to greater joy. Stop judging one another. Just allow each other to be. For, in the Universe that is what it is all about . . . just being, simply being . . . and forming no judgment of that.

Q. What is the appropriate thing to do when a couple is unable to reach an agreement on a meaningful issue?

First, make sure that it is a MEANINGFUL issue. We assume that you mean it is an issue involving integrity, particularly one's own integrity. If an issue is about being able to live within one's integrity, you have the opportunity to make choices. Do you want to change the issues surrounding your integrity? You can.

If you believe that it is not appropriate for you to change the issues surrounding your integrity, you have the opportunity to honor each other by altering the relationship. You can choose whether or not to stay in the relationship. You can choose to be friends or to go your separate ways.

There are choices in everything. There are options in everything. Existence is choices. Don't limit yourself. Don't bury yourself in a hole that you think you cannot move out of.

There is no dishonor in leaving relationships or in changing relationships. There is dishonor in staying in a relationship in which you cannot live within integrity. You must evaluate what is meaningful to you. If you both truly believe the issue is meaningful and you cannot reach agreement on it, then alter the relationship.

Q. Is it appropriate to terminate a relationship with a biological family member, that is, a parent, child, or sibling, when there are what appear to be irreconcilable differences?

We assume you mean this as a continuation of the last question, in which you talk about not being able to live within integrity in the relationship. It would be treated just as any other relationship would be treated. As we said, there is no shame in altering a relationship if it does not allow you to live within integrity.

Remember, you are not just a biological entity. You are ALSO an immortal life force. You are a dual entity. You are not bound by your biology.

Your biological family gave you an opportunity. Integrity encourages you to honor and respect that opportunity.

However, you are not tied to your biology by obligation or by rules and regulations any more than to any other relationship.

You have a history with these people. If you can continue within integrity in the relationship, it is joy. If you can't continue within integrity in the relationship, it does neither of you any good. Then you have to see how you can alter the relationship to accommodate the differences.

Q. Why do we feel as though we've failed when a relationship ends?

This is a very good question to ask upon the heals of these last two. To leave a relationship within integrity means that you still honor the other as a sacred soul on a sacred journey. You don't try to demean or hurt the other entity. You allow the other entity to be where he or she is.

It is important to remember that the other entity is always perfectly where he or she should be, because existence is evolutionary. It is a process of growth. To demean someone because that person is not at the same level of growth that you are is judgement. That is not honorable. But there is no shame in leaving a relationship when you treat the other entity with honor and respect.

Q. How are relationships going to change with the TRANSITION?

A great deal. Now much of your world exists in structures and systems that you have created — belief structures, philosophies, ways of doing things, laws, rules, and obligations — because of the corporeal body that serves as a tool in your existence.

When the TRANSITION takes place, your corporeal consistency will be altered. That will change a number of things. It is going to raise your consciousness. It is also going to give you an opportunity to heal YOURSELVES. You will not be relying on outside forces to either heal you emotionally or physically. Because of that, you are not going to have the same structural concepts. Consequently, there will be a greater feeling of freedom in relationships.

With this freedom, you will develop a greater realization of who you truly are. When this happens, you are going to be more capable of honoring one another, of understanding one another, and of not trying to bind one another down with obligations, rules, and systems.

You will not need to MAKE sense of things . . . because SENSE is going to be increased through CONSCIOUSNESS. Through this new found feeling of freedom, you will experience exhilaration and less need to control others. Even your society will let go of the need for control.

Q. If someone is now in a relationship with a person who is on approximately the same spiritual level, what are the chances of enjoying a meaningful relationship after the TRANSITION?

When you experience this TRANSITION into the next dimension, there are "steps" within that fourth dimension. There are still varying degrees of consciousness within that higher consciousness. You will find great compatibility in being with somebody who is near the same step you are experiencing.

There will still be challenges within this next dimension. It isn't as if everything is going to be "perfect." But you will have greater insight. You will be able to experience greater empathy. You will be able to read, understand, and feel other people's feelings to a greater degree.

Q. My current relationship woke up my desires — not just a desire for the person, but also a desire to achieve things that I had put on "hold." How is this so?

This can be the result of two people honoring each other. More importantly, when you honor yourself first in a relationship it allows the other person to honor himself or herself in the relationship. You are more fulfilled individuals. You have more to give to one another. You become a support system, a motivator, and an inspiration to your partner. There is no sense of competition. Competition may propel you to do things, but it is going to give you temporary results.

By inspiring within the other person the desire to be the greatest person that he or she can be, you are promoting a greater level of consciousness. You are helping that person raise his or her vibrations. That is what relationships are all about. If a relationship is not doing this — giving each other the space to grow and promoting honor and respect — then the relationship is not at the place it could be.

Q. I knew a man who was building a patio, but would never finish it. I could see that his wife was going through a tremendous amount of bearing up with this. It seemed as if he could never reach the end because if he reached the end, that would be the end. There was no growth. There was no accomplishment. There was only frustration. What was this all about?

This question actually concerns the "practice" of RESENTMENT in a relationship. When there is resentment in a relationship, it erodes the relationship. Instead of moving towards the goal, it is stepping away from the goal. When resentment is in a relationship, there will never be a happy ending.

When a relationship is in this state, it is because one of the partners in the relationship is not doing the best thing for himself. He may be giving in to the other person to make the other person happier, to keep the relationship together, or to keep from being yelled at, criticized, or condemned. Or he may be intentionally frustrating his partner to get "revenge."

What is most important in a relationship is to honor yourself by living according to those things that are the most important in your life — those things that make up your value · system. That is living within integrity. If you are giving up and giving in to things that are vitally important to your sense of integrity, then you are eroding not only yourself, you are eroding the relationship.·

Zachary, Sananda, & Ezekiel

DIMENSIONS

I knew my life force hadn't just crash landed here on Earth. I had prepared to come here. My cosmic memory told me that. My walks and talks in the ethereal realms with Transcendents verified that.

Nevertheless, I made mistakes just like everybody else. I made some poor decisions, got angry, lost my temper, banged a fender, gossiped, and committed a number of other faux pas. Now, why did I do that?

While I was nursing one of my wounds, the Transcendents gave me the answer to that question. They told me that I make mistakes for the same reason you do — because it's in the air. More accurately, it's in the dimension . . . specifically, the third dimension.

They showed me Paragraph 9, sub-section 12 of THE PLAN OF EXISTENCE, which we developed in cooperation with The Creator. This paragraph states: "All creators who are residents of the third dimensional level of consciousness will have as their greatest tool for advancing to the fourth dimension of consciousness the concept of DUALITY." (I'm kidding about the paragraph reference, but not the concept.)

I've come to understand that duality really means OPPOSITES — like happy and sad. As co-creators putting together THE PLAN, we knew that in order to be able to absorb the positive, higher vibrations like happiness and peace into our life forces, we needed to understand and reject their opposites — sadness and confusion.

We also knew it was not enough to conceptualize or understand the opposites mentally or intellectually. We knew we had to experience them. We knew that it was the FEELING we created through the experience that would raise our awareness and feed our life forces. That's really where the term "soul food" originated.

I've learned that more than anything duality is a way of thinking. One of the ways we are ensured the opportunity to participate in this way of thinking is by having human, corporeal bodies. That is because corporeal bodies have inherent physical challenges. It's by learning how to not-buy-into these physical challenges with our thinking that we advance to the next dimension of consciousness.

The Transcendents have told me that we begin the DANCE OF LIFE when our life force joins our human body on Earth. They advised me that the wise thing to do is to let our life force take the lead and encourage our body to follow. Regardless, the dance goes on in this dimension until we've produced enough positive vibrations to raise our life forces to the next dimension.

About 2,000 years ago, a being from another dimension came here to the Earth to teach us about the vibration known as ACCEPTANCE. This being, whom we named Jesus Christ, brought this vibration to us when we transitioned from the second to the third dimension of consciousness. The Spiritual Forces of the Universe anticipated that we would get ourselves stuck in the third dimension. So they sent Jesus to the Earth with the Universal Truth of Acceptance to help us move through the third and into the fourth dimension.

Just as the Spiritual Forces anticipated, we did get ourselves stuck in some duality foolishness known as "right-and-wrong." In fact, right-and-wrong became the most popular and powerful method for repressing the masses. It was used by individuals and institutions. It walked around in regal, religious, and tattered robes. It told people they were inherently "bad" because of "original sin." It created the concept of guilt — and guilt efficiently robbed people of their memory of themselves as creators and took away their dignity.

People killed to own this artificial concept of right-and-wrong because it represented power. Then right-and-wrong made these powerful people rich, and heartless, and stupid. It disempowered the rest of the people and made them acquiesce to sheer survival. It took away their dreams. It made them resentful, hateful, and violent. It created a two-edged sword called JUDGMENT that made mockery of those of the highest vibrations and consciousness. It almost always put those enlightened ones to death. In the process, right-and-wrong brought spiritual death to those who used it.

Most of us were born and raised under this banner of right-and-wrong. At the very least, we have had to live side-by-side with it. I know, it's been the most diligent companion I've had since I've been here. In my duality, I have even confessed, repressed, and at times regressed to keep it happy.

With the help of the Transcendents, however, I have

learned better. I have learned that we all have the ability and strength to step out of our third dimensional space suits . . . and out of this space of judgment and fear. When we do so, we will no longer plan our days to the tick-tock of a clock, nor tap our feet to the beat of measured music, nor be compelled to conform our attitudes to a place in time. We will let go of our need for right and wrong, good and bad. We will see existence for what it is — a space out of time.

In our higher consciousness, we will no longer embrace the status quo. We will view it as a temporary step, a point to grow from. We won't see suffering as "our due," nor view ourselves as victims any longer. We will remember who we are and embrace our experiences as our own creations . . . as opportunities . . . as stepping stones to the stars . . . back to our feeling of being ONE.

How is this so? This is also part of The Plan we helped create. We devised a system of MORE called DIMENSIONS.

We created eight dimensions in our Universe. We planned for each dimension to house a level of awareness known as CONSCIOUSNESS. Each level of consciousness was designed to be based on how well we knew ourselves as individuals and how well we knew ourselves as part of our collective Universe. The beings having the greatest level of awareness of SELF and ONE would reside in the eighth dimension.

We agreed that the different levels of consciousness would be identified by different levels of ENERGY VIBRATIONS. That way, as the co-creators advanced in consciousness, the vibrations of their life forces would become higher and lighter. As this happened, they would have greater access to the vibration known as JOY.

Life forces who function at the eighth dimensional level are very light and bright — more so than life forces in the first through seventh dimensions. In fact, life forces in the eighth dimension don't even have bodies as we know them. They don't need bodies like we do. They exist strictly as life forces. If they want to they can manifest a form that looks like ours. Their true form, however, is very different than the flesh, blood, and bones that structure our bodies. Again, their form is comprised of energy and light.

Here in the third dimensional Earth existence, we actually have two forms — a mortal human body AND an immortal life force. This is so we can fulfill the DUALITY clause in The Plan. Corporeal bodies are actually tools for experience in the first four dimensions of consciousness. After that, our consciousness is at a level of vibration that does not require their assistance.

The Plan also provides for the beings in the higher dimensions to be able to see and interact with the beings in the lower dimensions. That is so the more enlightened beings can assist the not-as-enlightened beings. In reality, a being in a dimension higher than you can be doing his or her thing right next to you and you probably wouldn't even know it.

There are some people in our dimension who have the ability to see into the higher dimensions at times. This ability exists for a number of reasons. The person may have developed this ability in a prior lifetime and brought it with him or her. The person may have developed the ability in this lifetime. Or the ability may have been brought with the person from another dimension, as in my case.

Duality has proven to be a worthy opponent, however. I must work very hard to maintain the level of vibrations I brought with me to the Earth. Otherwise, my abilities to see into the other dimensions are not consistent. Therefore, I use affirmations and exercises to keep my energy balanced. My walks and talks in the other dimensions also help my life force to maintain the lead in my dance of life.

The Transcendents also assist me on the Earth plane. Sometimes they even funnel concentrated energy into my body and life force. While this is not painful, it is excruciatingly uncomfortable. When they do this, I usually double over into a fetal position with stones or crystals in my hands until they are finished. This seems to help a bit with the discomfort. I just grin and bear the rest of the discomfort until the process is completed.

The results are worth it, though. I guarantee it! There is no other experience on the Earth that can compare with the knowledge, insight, peace, and intense joy that comes from these heightened vibrations.

As we TRANSITION from one dimension to the next, increasing levels of joy become the manna that feeds our life forces. Even now — as we are transitioning from the third to the fourth dimension — we are letting go of the confines of linear time and thinking and stepping into new vibrations . . . the joy of which we have never known before.

CHANNELING

The Nature of Time: Traveling Through Time & The Dimensions

Q. We are told that linear time does not exist in the higher dimensions. Why does linear time exist in the third dimensional Earth plane?

All, as you know it, and you don't know it, is part of a SYSTEM. This system emanates from The Creator and is a natural flow of organization, a natural flow of elements.

Part of this system is the stepping stones within it . . . the stepping stones through which entities go in order to return and manifest in the form of The Creator. Stepping stone three is what you call the third dimensional consciousness.

It is intended that, within this third dimensional consciousness there should exist DUALITY — left and right, east and west, yes and no, high and low — so that you, and The Creator through you, can experience DIFFERENCES. Linear time exists in your third dimension so you can experience duality and, therefore, differences.

Q. Can you tell us more about the nature of linear time?

Linear time is a mentality. It's a thought. That's all. This thought was placed in your corporeal DNA. It is literally a part of your mortal body, your humanness. It does not, however, exist in the mentality of your immortal life force.

Don't be put off by the limitations, as you see them, of your human body. They are only limitations insofar as you have not experienced anything else on Earth. But you have experienced other dimensions that do not have linear time, though you don't CONSCIOUSLY remember them. Therefore, you can transcend to some degree this essence of time that moves you. For, as awareness comes to you, your DNA alters and upgrades . . . and you can walk in other realities that do not have the limitations of linear time.

When you are able to do this, you will be considered "different." Don't be concerned about what other people think. Live your life as you know it is to be lived, as you want it to be lived. Live it to manifest yourself, to get to better know yourself, and to introduce yourself to The Creator.

Q. Is there another name for these other dimensions that don't have linear time?

We call it EXISTENCE. Once you are beyond this concept of linear time, you are just out there "doing existence."

Q. Can you describe for us what it is like to exist in a place or space that doesn't have linear time?"

We can. But for those of you who are tied to linear thinking, it may be somewhat difficult to understand.

If you had experienced the joy of unconditional love even for a second in your life — and that's usually how long it lasts on the human plane — then you would understand how VIBRATIONS actually change your essence and your feelings.

Even a second of experiencing the higher vibration of unconditional love opens a doorway for you into dimensions where life and existence merely exist. They are not judged. They are lived. They are experienced. They are fluid. They are a part of the pathway that leads you back to that full realization of being The Creator.

This is a space where one can experience greater group consciousness because there is not the necessity to judge, to feel guilty, nor to be hateful. It is that space of ACCEPTANCE.

Q. How is it possible to know the joy and value of living with "no-time" when we live in the third dimensional Earth plane?

It is difficult unless you are willing to let go of convention, tradition, rules, regulations, and expectations. When you are willing to exist without all of this paraphernalia and, particularly, without the concern of what others think of you, you are capable of experiencing this space of "no-time."

This requires a severing from others while maintaining a knowledge of oneness with those others. Once you can understand how you can be separate and still a part of the whole, you're ready to experience this space of existence without linear time.

Q. We are told that what we call past, present, and future are occurring simultaneously. How can this be?

You look at things in a historical, linear perspective upon the Earth plane. That serves a purpose for you — it helps you to grow upon what you see as your past. Take that belief and turn it upside down.

The most important thing to understand is that what you understand is not ALL THAT IS. It is only part of ALL THAT IS. It is a temporary stopover. You are at a rest stop, so to speak, and this part of existence is what's happening at this rest stop. But it's only happening at this rest stop.

When you understand the existence of OVERSOULS, this concept is easier to visualize. Just as The Source Creator's life force severed into myriads of co-creators to overcome the "limitations of one," so your own individual life force may have severed into a number of other expressions of yourself. These other expressions of yourself are known as oversouls.

Just as you are related to The Creator, you are uniquely tied to your oversouls through cosmic DNA. The purpose of having oversouls — to make the most of your unique existence — is enabled through this cosmic DNA. Thereby, the experiences and learnings of each of your oversouls become part of YOUR consciousness and the consciousness of ALL of your other oversouls.

Your oversouls can exist in other times and dimensions simultaneously with you. They can also manifest in the same time and dimension with you.

Q. We are told that we can travel through time to the past and future. Please explain how this can happen.

You're only limited by your thoughts! You have been programmed to think past, present, and future. You have been told that you can live in only one of these existences at a time. Transcend that thinking!

Understand that even as you sleep, even as you daydream, even as you rest at times, your conscious self goes into a state of being not-conscious. In that state, you are not fearful, nor are you bound by tradition, contradictions, or teachings that are incomplete. In that state, your consciousness spreads its supraconscious wings and goes to all of these different simultaneous existences.

Understand that you all do this. That is part of your existence on Earth — a part very few people understand, accept, or embrace. It is your reality that you are not bound here to the Earth plane, to this single existence. You have wings to fly to other simultaneous existences which you call time.

The key is to get so smart and so over it that you can do it when you're CONSCIOUS.

Conscious time is based upon level of consciousness. If you want to make interdimensional and time travel an integral part of your life, make the pursuit of consciousness your path. When you honestly work towards that in both your humanness and your life forceness, this process will become natural to you.

Use the process you call meditation to help you get to the jumping off point into simultaneous existences and other dimensions.

Q. Is it beneficial for us to travel in time and/or dimensions? If so, why?

It can be if you don't get lost in it — not lost in the

sense of directional loss and not being able to get back to yourself — but lost in the dynamics of it all so that you don't want to come back and perform your function on Earth. For, when you experience a higher dimension of consciousness and its greater vibrations, it is difficult to walk amongst heavier vibrations again . . . especially in a consciousness that does not embrace the higher principles of the system.

As long as your ability to travel to simultaneous existences and through dimensions promotes your mission or your purpose on Earth, then it is of value. If it detracts from your mission or purpose, it is not of value.

That sounds like enlightenment.

. . . A very good word for it.

Q. What's the difference between traveling in time and traveling in the dimensions?

"Dimensions" is another word for CONSCIOUSNESS. As the creators travel through existence, they come to better understand themselves and what the purpose of their existence is. The more they understand and live what they understand, the more they raise their consciousness. As their consciousness raises, they literally change from one reality to another reality. Those realities are called dimensions.

What you call time is really SIMULTANEOUS EXISTENCE. Simultaneous existence means that the past, present, and future are all existing at the SAME time. Simultaneous existence can actually take place in the same dimension that you're in or in other dimensions. So you may have oversouls who are living simultaneously with your NOW but doing it in other dimensions of consciousness and in other spaces of time.

Work to understand and develop your "oneness connection" with your oversouls. Work to visit and travel with your oversouls. Work to share and communicate with your oversouls, as well as with the transcendent forces.

Q. What process do we use to travel in time and dimensions?

Process is separate from vehicle. The VEHICLE that you use to travel in simultaneous existences and in dimensions is your life force. Your life force has no limitations outside of the body it inhabits. You need to learn how to allow your life force, your vehicle, to separate temporarily from your corporeal bodies to accomplish this. The PROCESS is learning how to accomplish this separation.

Q. Is there anything else it would be appropriate for us to know about this concept of time?

You've got the basics. You've got the framework. Now go out and DO this. Go out and live this.

How *do you do* this? You *do* it through this thing called meditation. You *do* it through prayer. You *do* it through letting go of the limitations of the human brain by being with a sunset or a sunrise or in a space of love with a partner. You *do* this by reading; by groups such as the spiritual development meeting you're in now; by talking to others; by taking classes and workshops; but, mostly by living according to who you know you REALLY are.

Zachary, Sananda, & Ezekiel

ALWAYS

Dearest Zachary,

Magic! That is what you have brought to my life . . . sprinkled with diplomacy, non-judgment, no-fear, and the joy of awareness.

Since you "came aboard" (as you put it) in 1993, you have been my mentor and guardian. You promised me then that you would be with me always, and you have honored that commitment one hundred percent. Every minute of every day has been filled with your wisdom and companionship, your words and wit, your light and incredible love. Your pure vibrations touch the depth of my very being. I could not feel you more in my life if I could touch your ethereal face with my human hands.

You have spoken to me in words I can hear, pictures I can see, scents I can smell, and experiences I can feel in my heart and soul. These experiences have stirred "knowingness" in my ethereal mind. We have traveled together many times to where there is ALL THAT IS. You've given me much information from there to brighten and enlighten the lives of others upon the Earth. Through your spiritual participation in our lives, we are remembering that we are ONE with each other . . . with our BROTHERS AND SISTERS IN THE SKY . . . with The Creator. We are remembering who we are, where we are from, and why we are here.

Though you refer to me as "Little One," you have taught me my power. As I stood in front of you, Ezekiel, and Sananda in Council and argued my case for our beloved Starseed, you did not resent the intrusion of my opinion. You honored my awareness. I find it an incredible lesson that those of higher consciousness don't discount the opinions of others . . . that the essence of AWARENESS is ACCEPTANCE. What a joy experiencing this reality has brought into my life.

I know your intent has always been my betterment. Yet you have asked for nothing in return. You gave me my life on Pleiades and now you bring me quality of life on planet Earth. You have ignited in me the memory of my Pleiadian identity and of time spent with you and mother, uncle Zachariah, my wonderful brothers and sisters, and our own "little ones."

I have experienced a peace beyond all understanding as the result of knowing that my identity extends beyond the limitations of a human body and into the vast capabilities of the Universe — that I have accessible to me the healing of the Sirians, the balanced male-female energy of the Andromedans, the music and art of the Arcturians, the brilliant systems and technology of the Orions, and the integrity of the Hakubahns.

Most of all, Zachary, I am thankful for knowing that even though technology is limited, consciousness is not . . . that through the vehicle of HIGHER CONSCIOUSNESS and NO-EGO, we can literally travel through time, dimension, and space. As you well know, if the Earth's World Government appropriated its time, money, and energy to raising the consciousness of the citizens of Earth instead of on developing propulsion systems, they would already be acquainted with their brothers and sisters in the sky.

At times, when the day-to-day third dimensional pressures are so demanding, confusing, and full of heart-ache, I wonder why I would have volunteered to be a part of introducing those on Earth to their brothers and sisters in the sky. But when you remind me of What Really Is and I feel your unconditional love and support, I am glad for the opportunity. For, there is nothing greater in all of our Universe than knowing who we are and what part we play in ALL THAT IS. What a gift you have given me — and what a lesson you have taught me — in allowing me to be thankful for the errors in my thinking instead of feeling foolish for my ignorance.

My heart-felt intent is for this book to reach the hearts and minds of those who are ready to recognize that they are citizens of a Universe filled with sentient life and limitless potential. But most of all, I look forward to their recognizing the limitations of technology and appropriately choosing their exploration of the heavens to be in VEHICLES OF HIGHER CONSCIOUSNESS.

I will ALWAYS love you dearly.
Your Daughter,

Janis

CHANNELING

Your Attitude Is Your Prayer

Q. Here on Earth, we think of PRAYER as a one-way communication with "God." We usually use prayer to ask for assistance of one kind or another. Is prayer a universal concept? If so, how does it differ from our concept on Earth?

JAN: The Creator is joining us. (S)he is asking me to interpret because some of the information is symbolic and pictorial.

The Creator says that the beginning of prayer was at the beginning of creation. Prayer was part of THE PLAN to have all of us stay connected to one another, so we would never forget that we are all ONE.

Prayer is literally a communication system, whereby we are capable of communicating one with the other over long distances, even insofar as between planets. It is closely related to those processes that we on Earth call "channeling" and "interdimensional travel." It is also akin to that process we call "empathing," whereby we can know what is happening with somebody at extraordinary distances.

Q. Has the process or form of prayer changed over time?

(The Transcendents speaking) Much! Even more than over time, however, the process varies throughout the dimensions.

Prayer is a much different process in the first dimension than it is in the eighth dimension. In the first dimension, you are just beginning to experience yourselves. You literally experience yourselves through reaching out and TOUCHING another person. As you transition upward through the dimensions — to where the corporeal body form has no existence and only the ethereal life force exists — there only needs to be the process of THOUGHT to communicate one with the other.

Q. Is there any one particular process we should follow now when praying?

Use the process that works best for you in realizing your connection to the WHOLE — to The Creator and to one another — and helps you to experience UNCONDITIONAL LOVE. If that is through meditation, then meditation is a prayer. If that is through outward speaking, then that is the process that is appropriate for you. There is no one process. There is only the process that works best for you.

Q. Is there anything else that would be appropriate for us to know about this concept that we call prayer?

Remember, prayer is communicating, not only with The Creator, but with one another. It has no limitations.

In your dimension, the concept of prayer is very much linked to your corporeal body form. In reality, to magnify your ability for successful prayer, your best opportunity is to step outside of your corporeal thinking to communicate one with the other. Then, you will be able to experience prayer as a manifestation of unconditional love.

Those things that you manifest in existence are only limited by the power of your thought. So it is with prayer. Prayer is only limited by the power of your thought. Think big. When you recognize that, you will know that your prayers become universal through the power of your thoughts.

Q. What is the significance of the Lord's Prayer given in the Bible? Some of it seems to be a little difficult for me.

Prayer is significant only when it comes from the center, the life force, the heart, the true essence of the entity communicating it. For anyone other than the creator of a prayer, there is usually little significance.

If you FEEL a significant connection to the words or

essence of this prayer, then it is appropriate for you. But you are the only one who can determine its significance for you.

There are "levels" of communication. It is up to you to decide how clear you want your communication to be. For maximum effect, you want to adjust your "prayer" radio to the channel that reaches out most HONESTLY, that creates the CLEAREST link of communication, and that generates the strongest feeling of UNCONDITIONAL LOVE. That will include the content and form that is most appropriate for YOU.

Q. Are you saying that self-honesty and acceptance without judgement are a form of prayer?

(Sananda speaking) The purpose of my coming to this Earth was to bring you a higher level of consciousness — one in which you would be able to successfully master the PRINCIPLE OF ACCEPTANCE. You accomplish that through the process of non-judgment and through LIVING the Principle of Acceptance.

Is not your attitude a prayer? And is not your life lived upon this attitude of prayer? So then, yes, self-honesty and acceptance without judgment are a form of prayer.

The Creator,
Zachary, Sananda, & Ezekiel

HUMAN RADIOS

Radios. What a concept. By turning a knob or pushing a button on a radio, we can surf vibratory frequencies to hear music, news, advertisements, and advice on daily living. We can tune into Ohio, New York, Chicago, London, or even Berlin. In fact, we can travel over these frequencies to almost anywhere in the world.

People are like radios. They come in all sizes and colors and with a variety of options. They're a storehouse of information and feelings. And all that incredible knowledge and those feelings have vibratory frequencies.

As fate may have it, I find myself able to tune into these "human" frequencies. I use the word "fate" loosely here. In fact, part of the two and one-half years of preparation for my soul exchange with Cassy included fine tuning my own frequencies to be capable of doing this.

It is a profound experience to walk in someone else's shoes. Here in these frequencies, I am able to do just that — to be with another person's thoughts and feelings. Here in these frequencies, we truly become one. There is no need to cover up feelings or manipulate words. Communication supersedes words. For here there is complete acceptance. It is a place of no-judgment and total honesty.

To understand how this is possible, you must understand that all life forces are multi-dimensional. Basically, this means that your body can be in one place and your life force can be in another. In all honesty, it's a rather difficult concept to understand unless you have consciously experienced it. I put emphasis on the word CONSCIOUSLY because you most certainly have experienced multi-dimensional travel. You just may not remember it. Trust me. I guarantee this is so.

Multi-dimensionality is an inherent ability of your life force. The first time you consciously experience it with your human body, you may think you're ready for a straight jacket. The more you experience it, the more natural it becomes. After a while, the trips to the grocery store, gas station, doctor's office, and work are what become unreal. In fact, "reality" is a dynamic, fascinating subject in itself, and one which we discuss quite often throughout the book. Suffice it to say, there are a lot of things you're capable of that you don't yet understand.

I'm going to call this ability to surf the human frequencies EMPATHING. Many of you, too, are capable of empathing. In fact, I sometimes walk my clients and Starseed group through this experience. Fundamentally, this is what I have them do:

Step 1:   Turn on your POWER/CONSCIOUSNESS button.

Step 2:   Switch from **Automatic Method** (conscious awareness beta brain waves) to

Fine-tuned Method (an altered state of consciousness/theta brain waves) through a process like meditation.

Step 3:   Adjust your graphic equalizer to filter out FEAR and JUDGMENT.

Step 4:   Select the channel (person's life force) you want to tune into.

Step 5:   Adjust your VOLUME/*SENSITIVITY* so you can hear the person. **

Step 6:   Listen with your HEART.

Step 7:   Repeat Steps 1-6 over and over again.

** NOTE: NEVER skip Step 5. If you skip this step, you will not be able to complete your connection. If you are unable to adjust your SENSITIVITY so you can hear, repeat Step 3. If you still cannot connect, run a diagnostic on your level of self-absorption. Upgrade your COMPASSION module. Adjust your thinking. Repeat steps 1-6.

Why is SENSITIVITY so important? Because that's what existence is all about.

Earlier in the book, we heard The Creator call us his/her

FOOTSTEPS. The Creator manifested a holographic Universe for all of us to walk in. That means we were created in the virtual image of the Creator. Each and every one of us is a COMPLETE creator. Everything we, as an individual creator, think, feel, and do, becomes part of the existence of The Source Creator and our co-creators. It feeds the Collective of Creators. It is eternally creating our COLLECTIVE CONSCIOUSNESS. This cannot not be.

Now, if we are a collective consciousness, we are ONE. When I look at you, I see myself and vice-versa. We mirror each other's achievements, lessons needing to be learned, negativity, positivity, everything.

In order to know yourself, it is necessary for you to understand the other creators. To understand "the others," you need to understand their thoughts and feelings. Whether or not you agree with those thoughts and feelings is irrelevant. All you need to do is allow your fellow creators the dignity of being at their own level of consciousness.

Sensitivity is the vibratory frequency that allows you to be with the thoughts and feelings of the other creators. Sensitivity is how you learn to understand them.

You are not designed to be an island unto yourself. Despite the fact that relationships with the other creators can be challenging and hurtful, they're necessary. They're your opportunity to adjust your sensitivity frequency (Step 5 above).

Sensitivity requires courage. When you are sensitive, you are more likely to suffer from the negative thoughts and feelings of others. There's no need to worry, though. You have a built-in self-regeneration system — your life force.

Besides, fielding some negative energy is a small price to pay for understanding when that understanding comes with "The Big J" — JOY! Joy is also a frequency. Nothing looks better and feels better than joy.

On one of my multi-dimensional journeys with Zachary, I had an experience that brought me face-to-face with the reality of our NEED for sensitivity. I hope you will enjoy the wisdom in this short excursion too.

Zachary and I are moving very quickly over an area. It's beautiful. There's blue water, blue skies, and beautiful white beaches. When I ask him where we are, he tells me this place is Antarctica.

"But this isn't what Antarctica looks like," I tell him.

"This is the way it is intended to look," he responds. "It is the hardness, the coldness of your hearts that have turned it into such. And so it is in the third dimension."

Janis Abriel

The beauty and the beast of relationships with the other creators is DIFFERENCES.

My ability to empath first manifested in response to my clients' needs for assistance in resolving differences in their relationships. I discovered if my clients could see matters from the perspective of "the other," they were able to either mend and improve their relationships or make an appropriate decision to part peacefully. This empath process, according to my clients, has been an invaluable resource in their relationships . . . perhaps one of the most popular and helpful spiritual processes I perform.

I've discovered that the quality of my empathing is dependent upon the quality of my sensitivity. Since sensitivity manifests itself in COMPASSIONATE BEHAVIOR, I've learned to assess my sensitivity by observing my behavior.

If I offer "constructive criticism" (by the way, there's no such thing as CONSTRUCTIVE criticism) to an excessively slow sales clerk, it's not a good day to empath. Why? Because criticism of any kind is an assumption of superiority. Compassion has no element of inferiority or superiority. Compassion sees everyone as equal — the one in need of compassion is supreme. Compassion is a blessed OPPORTUNITY to help relieve the suffering of that SUPREME BEING.

It is performing those supreme acts of compassion that gives us a profound view of life and creates sacred covenants between us. We may not be able to see those covenants, but they manifest in our ability to connect with the thoughts and feelings of our fellow human beings.

CHANNELING

Compassion & Enlightenment

Q. Please describe for us the nature of this attitude and activity we here on the Earth call COMPASSION.

We, too, have such an attitude and activity. We call it GETTING ALONG. We call it SHARING. We call it LOVING. We call it HIGHER CONSCIOUSNESS.

Compassion stems from unconditional love — not love — but, UNCONDITIONAL love. To be compassionate, one must work out of one's life force. That life force is the part of you that generates and absorbs unconditional love.

Compassion is an aspect of enlightenment. For when one is capable of being compassionate, one is capable of stepping off of your Earth and into the stars.

Compassion is something that touches the hearts of your people but very few practice it. We do so much appreciate even the small acts of compassion that are carried out on your Earth. None of it is overlooked. None of it is missed. We know everything that transpires.

We know when you display compassion and caring — a

true caring out of wanting nothing back, out of giving in an unconditional way — because it fills you as well as the other person. This is one of those times when it is okay to want something for yourself. One of the greatest aspects of compassion is that you know when you are being filled yourself by the act that you perform, you are doing ten times that for the other person . . . and a hundred times that for your group consciousness.

Compassion is something that should be part of your GROUP consciousness. On your Earth, compassion is shown in more solitary acts. As you move into the higher dimensions, those acts will be prompted by your collective attitude.

Compassion knows nothing of judgment. Compassion knows nothing of guilt. Compassion is total acceptance of anybody in any state and stature of life.

Compassion is wanting only the best for a person and doing everything that you can to help that person in every way. It is helping that person to grow in such a way that he or she does not continue to be bound to acts that cause suffering, pain, or challenge, but promotes acts that build joy and bring happiness.

Q. Is compassion an attitude and activity valued throughout the Universe? Would it be considered a Universal Truth?

Absolutely! Compassion is valued throughout the dimensions. Have we not talked before about unconditional love and joy being vibrations and how these vibrations feed our life forces? These vibrations also feed expressions of compassion.

Is it not compassion that brings us to you? Do we need to be here? No. We do not need to be here. We are here because we love you and want to serve you.

Q. Where is it appropriate to draw the line between compassion and being an "enabler." That is, how does one practice compassion without disempowering the recipient of one's compassion?

That is an issue for you because of the DUALITY in your existence. At one end of the continuum you have compassion, and at the other end of the continuum you have disempowerment. So, where does one draw the line? One clue is when the other person says to you, "Stop, I need to make my own decisions." Listen when your intuition tells you that what you are doing is making that person dependent upon you.

Another clue is if the EGO is involved. Is the other person's ego involved? Is your ego involved? Are you doing this because it somehow feeds you? If you are feeding off of acts of compassion, they are not acts of compassion. They are acts of disempowerment. For you to be performing acts out of your own personal needs disempowers YOU as well as the other person.

Look at what we talk about. Look at ego. Look at intent. LISTEN to the other person. Listen to other people as well, for they have very good advice on those things. Ultimately, however, what it comes down to is listening to your own life force . . . listening to that which you call your intuition or your higher self. That is how you will know.

Much of your society has suffered because of the need of one segment to control and the others to follow. You have "controllers" and you have "sheep." To us, it is pretty obvious when this is the situation. For you, the distinctions are much more subtle. Learn about these distinctions. Listen to the people who have the insight into this. Learn about this issue that you call CONTROL. For understanding this issue is key to the answer you are looking for.

Q. Is lack of compassion related to acts of abuse and violence?

Abuse and violence exist because of the issue of control. BEING OUT OF CONTROL or FEELING OUT OF CONTROL are the roots of abuse and violence. Also at issue are not having learned to behave otherwise, lacking self-esteem, and lacking the self-control necessary to conduct one's life in BALANCE.

A person functioning out of ego and needing, therefore, to function only within areas under his or her own control will not have the ability to act compassionately. That person is more prone to acts of violence and abuse. This is a simplification, of course, because there are many other factors that build acts of abuse and violence. But key to part of those issues of abuse and violence is behavior born of ego instead of SELF-ESTEEM.

Q. Compassion seems to be an expression of the FEMALE energy. Why is this so?

It is as The Creator wanted it. Compassion helps integrate the female energy into the male energy. For example, sometimes a nut and a bolt don't fit together very well. What you might do is put some oil or graphite on the nut so the bolt goes into the nut. This is similar to using compassion to help integrate the male and female energies.

Q. There are some people on Earth who appear to lack the ability to act compassionately. We refer to this form of behavior here on Earth as narcissism. We have two questions regarding this:

♦ *First, what is the root of this apparent lack of*

*compassion? Is it in any way related to the phenomenon
we call SELFISHNESS?*

Selfishness is a manifestation of the same root as lack
of compassion.

Those people in your dimension who seem to lack this
ability for compassion — who are self-serving, and so much so
that they don't have the desire or energy to step outside of
themselves to serve another — is caused from a number of
things. Basically, the root is LOWER CONSCIOUSNESS. This feeds
both that thing you call selfishness and that thing you call
narcissism. You sometimes refer to it as having "dull karmic
roots" — those people who have not developed themselves over
lifetimes and, therefore, have lower vibrations.

♦   *Second, is it possible for someone to be completely void
of the capability of expressing compassion? If so, how
can this be?*

Nobody is void of the CAPABILITY, but some people are
void of the PROBABILITY.

Those people who have been brought up in a society, or
in families, or in some kind of an arrangement where they have
not been taught the value of compassion — where they have
never seen compassion, where they have been physically or

verbally abused, where they have been criticized, condemned, or constantly complained at — tend to have a lesser propensity for compassion. If they are busy licking their own wounds, it is very difficult for them to lick somebody else's. They don't have the time. They don't have the energy. They don't have the inclination.

They may also manifest a lesser capability for compassion because of remembrances they brought into this existence from other lifetimes.

Q. We felt that Princess Diana and Sister Theresa were icons of compassion. If this is so, why did they incarnate at THIS time in Earth's history?

You spoke tonight about compassion being linked to ACCEPTANCE. In order to fulfill your third dimensional consciousness, the GROUP consciousness of the Principle of Acceptance must be brought to fruition. So it was that the examples of Diana and Sister Theresa were given to you on the eve of your TRANSITION into the fourth dimension.

Q. Is there anything we have not addressed in these questions that would be appropriate for us to know about this attitude and activity we refer to on the Earth as compassion?

Don't UNDERESTIMATE the power of compassion and don't OVERESTIMATE your power. Compassion requires humility. There is no place for ego in compassion. There is no place for senselessness in compassion. One needs to have humility and sensibility to understand the power of compassion.

One act of compassion can change a person's life completely. So never underestimate the effect that you can have on your society through your acts of compassion. Build one act of compassion upon the other until it becomes an integral vibration in your own existence.

Q. Is ENLIGHTENMENT the same thing as CONSCIOUSNESS? Please give us a definition of enlightenment.

Enlightenment is like the light bulb going on in your head. You know how you feel when you hear something and say, "I get that! It makes everything else that I have learned make sense." That is what enlightenment is. It is taking all the things that you know exist in your subconscious and supraconscious and bringing them to your consciousness.

So, enlightenment is connected to consciousness . . . and then DOING something with it. It is using the supraconscious to pull your subconscious into your consciousness and then using that consciousness in com-passionate, loving, caring ways — ways that build people and help them evolve into their own greater consciousness.

Q. How does one achieve enlightenment? Or does one ever achieve enlightenment?

Enlightenment is a process, just as everything else is. We have said before that there is always a god's god. Enlightenment may be an "I got it!" but it never ends with that. It is continual. It goes on and on. You may have an incident of enlightenment. You may have a period of enlightenment. But ultimately there is always the PROCESS of enlightenment.

Q. What role do DUALITY and CHALLENGE play in the process of attaining enlightenment?

They make you fight to get there because you don't want to experience pain. They motivate you to seek higher, greater, and better things in your life. And the greatest thing that one can seek is consciousness, or enlightenment, as you call it.

Q. Does enlightenment bring peace of mind to the practitioner?

Not always. As one becomes more enlightened, one becomes also more aware of how much further there is to go . . . not only for oneself . . . but for other individuals and for the group consciousness. So enlightenment can bring an anguish with it, too — an anguish of wanting to give people more and knowing that they are not ready for it. At the same time, enlightenment brings one the ability to ACCEPT. So enlightenment is a balance of peace of mind and anguish.

Q. Is there validity, then, to the belief that ignorance is bliss?

When one is un-enlightened, one has very little concern for other people. It is concern for other people that causes us to go out there and become involved with the other people. It is the involvement with other people that brings the challenges.

To exist in solitary does not bring challenge. It also does not bring growth. But being involved with others does. It also brings grief. It brings anguish. It brings pain. So ignorance and lack of awareness allow one to go throughout existence in a state of NON-EXISTENCE, so to speak. But this is not a happy place to be. It is just a void place to be.

Ignorance is settlement. Ignorance is non-feeling. It does not give one a sense of bliss. It gives one a sense of emptiness. But if one is empty of suffering and pain, one is also empty of joy, laughter, and happiness.

Q. Is there anything else that is appropriate for us to understand about enlightenment that we have not already addressed in our questions?

We would like to reiterate that enlightenment is a process. Don't fall into those thinkings that say you should feel guilty for not being enlightened. You are doing enlightenment at your own pace. Everybody is moving forward — some like snails, others like rocket ships. Nevertheless, everybody is moving forward.

So, don't let others control, or manipulate, or disempower you by telling you that you are not enlightened. Don't accept that. You are just enlightenment in the making.

Zachary, Sananda, & Ezekiel

RETIRED HUMAN RADIOS

I really related to Whoopi Goldberg in the movie *Ghost*. Until her deceased partner-in-rectifying-crime got her to spit the word "ditto" out of her mouth, her credibility was zilch with his wife. In fact, most people think people who talk to "dead people" (Whoopi's words) are just a notch above totally insane.

When I first started empathing (also known as medium communications) with "dead people" — sensing, seeing, and hearing them — I didn't understand much more about the nature of death than Whoopi did. I did know I wasn't involved in a mainstream activity.

As I spent more and more time communicating with these **RETIRED HUMAN RADIOS**, I discovered that they're just like everybody else, with one significant exception. When they lay their mortal bodies aside and proceed through the portal of death and into The Light, their frequencies change. All negative programming, such as anger, resentment, and fear is upgraded to **WISDOM** by the higher vibrations of their new home. The result is delightful.

They can be witty, charming, humorous, direct, profound, or whatever else their ethereal personalities are feeling. They enjoy sharing the details of their dynamic existence on the **OTHER SIDE OF LIFE** with us. They talk about their goals, career tracks, and relationships. Because they have stepped out of the LITTLE PICTURE framed by corporeal existence, they are outstanding teachers, as well. I love talking to them!

I have taken giant strides forward in understanding life and living as the result of my lively conversations with these teachers from the other side — the young father of three small children, the teenage boy who committed suicide, the elderly man who lived a fulfilling life, and the hundreds of others so willing to share to help me and those they left behind.

Two of these retired human radios, in particular, stand out in my mind. That is because they shared, through their dramatic stories, what I consider to be one of the most important universal truths — judgment is a temporary, human creation. It does not exist as a universal principle.

The first of these two, a famous woman who died mercilessly at the hands of her ex-husband, told me that she had no need for retribution. In response to my surprise, she explained to me that on the other side of life there is no duality. In the absence of a corporeal body, the life force has no need to satisfy the dualistic demands present on the Earth plane. That is, crime does not need to be balanced by punishment. She assured me that the Earth plane would exact its own form of justice to balance the scales of duality, even though this was no longer any of her concern. She then explained to me the necessity of looking at all human activities in two ways — by way of the LITTLE PICTURE *and* the BIG PICTURE.

The LITTLE PICTURE is of our material existence. Among other things, this picture includes our corporeal body, our residence, our car, the food we eat, our job, our recreation, and our trips to the grocery store, dentist, and post office. It is the world in which we develop, test, and re-assess our values. It is our opportunity to fulfill the experiences we pre-destined for ourselves before entering the Earth plane, the experiences we choose during the course of our living, and the experiences manifested through the collective consciousness we associate with — our family, our friends, our career, our philosophies, our institutions, our community, our nation, and our planet. The LITTLE PICTURE is the world in which we learn how to balance the scales of duality — love and indifference, happy and sad, strength and weakness, justice and dishonor, freedom and fear, crime and punishment — in order to understand who we REALLY are. It is the world of our mortality.

The BIG PICTURE is of our ethereal existence. Among other things, this picture includes our life force, our relationship to The Creator and all the other co-creators, specific "soul groups," and interdimensional trips and conversations. It is the world of energy and vibrations. It is the manifestation of unconditional love, joy, self-knowing, embraced differences, limitless possibilities, and creation from thought. It is the playground of gods and the breeding ground of *there is forever MORE*. It is the world of our immortality. It is who we REALLY are.

As this famous woman (I'll call her Marla) explained to me, in the LITTLE PICTURE she was considered a victim. Her death was viewed as an atrocity, a crime of the greatest proportions. For the people involved — her ex-husband (I'll call him Bill), families, friends, police, the justice system, and on-lookers — it was a monumental challenge to figure out what punitive actions would be used to balance the scales of justice.

In the **BIG PICTURE**, Marla told me, she and Bill had chosen this experience before even setting foot on the Earth. They knew in that space before they reincarnated that the collective consciousness on the Earth was having severe difficulties honoring differences. In fact, honor was being distributed disproportionately in a pecking order according to gender, race, age, status, and species. One of the repercussions of this enterprise was that males were beating, maiming, raping, and killing females, especially their "beloveds," and society was often turning its collective head.

Marla and Bill wanted to upgrade this collective thinking in a **BIG** way. So they devised a plan. They decided they would incarnate around the same linear time on Earth, meet, marry, have children, and divorce. Marla would then die violently at Bill's hands and he would be tried publicly in the third dimensional justice system of duality for the world to witness.

Marla assured me that she was satisfied with the results of their plan. The people of the Earth were in the process of raising their collective standard of thinking about domestic violence. The third dimensional justice system would exact its price over a period of time to achieve the necessary balance.

The families were on a path to higher consciousness, spurred by the insights generated from their personal suffering. And Marla and Bill had fulfilled their spiritual commitment to one another.

Marla opened another doorway to understanding for me, as well. She told me that she honored Bill's immortal life force for the courage it took to implement this plan. He knew when the plan was developed that he would suffer extensively at the hands of society and his own conscience for the rest of his life on the physical plane. Marla told me that quite often the entities who appear to be our antagonists, even our enemies, are IN REALITY our beloved soul mates. So it was with Marla and Bill.

Over time I have applied this BIG PICTURE principle to many specific situations. It has become an invaluable tool in making sense of the sometimes nonsensical world we seem to live in.

About a year ago, I had the opportunity to communicate with a being who had died on the Earth plane at the hands of her mother. At the time of her death, she (I'll call her Sara) was five months old. She shared this amazing picture with me.

Sara's mother had been suffering from postpartum psychosis since Sara's birth. She started abusing Sara almost immediately and the abuse escalated over the next months. When Sara's mother realized she couldn't control or stop her rage, she sought professional help. A psychiatrist prescribed medication for her but took no other steps to intervene in

Sara's behalf. Sara's father was not even notified of the abuse. Obviously, this course of action didn't work.

During Sara's final beating, as her head was being hit against a counter top, angels surrounded her. They stroked her and talked to her, distracting her from the experience. Filled with their presence, she experienced virtually no pain or trauma. The angels took her home to The Light in a state of complete peace.

When I met Sara, her ethereal form was that of a young woman. Her golden hair fell to her shoulders. She had a radiant smile and appeared like an angel herself.

Sara told me that she spent several hours every day sitting next to her mother in the prison cell. She desperately wanted her mother to be able to see her and hear her, but she couldn't. Sara's words to me were, "I can see my mother suffering . . . so much more than I ever did." She wanted her mother to know that she bore no grudge. She wanted to help ease her mother's suffering.

Sara told me that this lesson had also been pre-destined by the participants — her mother, father, grandparents, and her parents' friends — to force them to deal with their past, denial, pedophilia, co-dependency, ego, and drug abuse.

Sara also reinforced for me that there is no need for judgment on the other side of life. The "saint" and the "sinner" are welcomed alike there.

Our family and friends on the other side of life view the Earth as a stage. They tell me that each one of us writes our own "play of life" before we set foot on this stage. We manifest our own realities based upon a truly supernatural connection we have with higher consciousness. We just consciously forget about that connection when the curtain opens on our play at birth — when we begin playing out the experiences we ourselves pre-destined in the scripts we wrote.

Are we locked into this "pre-destination?" Those on the other side assure me we are not. Our inalienable cosmic birthright as citizens of the Universe guarantees that we are decision makers. This birthright — free agency — ensures our ability to manifest our choices. Therefore, we can re-write the scripts of our lives at any time if we so choose.

These retired human radios are a LIVING example of what they tell us — that we are more than our human bodies. Each of us is an indispensable part of the BIG PICTURE.

Immediately following this page, you will find some information shared with me by my deceased uncle, Dick, regarding the nature of death. Then you will find a medium communication I had with Diana, "The People's Princess" of Wales, who left the Earth plane on August 31, 1997. Both give further personal incites into the BIG PICTURE of existence.

But before you turn this page, I want to share one more thing with you — the knowing I have of the peace that comes from realizing that death is of no consequence to those who experience it. The challenge of death is left to the living . . . and that is a challenge we can all deal with by accepting that our loved ones are alive and well in another dimension of our existence.

DEATH IS FOR THE LIVING

Information Shared from
the Other Side of Life
by Janis Abriel's
Uncle Dick

In memory of his life here
1918-1993

When we lay aside life
on the Earth plane, we have
the opportunity to make a very important decision. At the
instant of death, we can mentally accept our new state of
being and be embraced in its wonder, or we can refuse to
accept this new state of being and live in a world between life
and death known as the astral plane. Death, thereby, becomes
a STATE OF MIND.

After death, we go to what Uncle Dick fondly calls the
HOLDING TANK and describes as being absolutely grand. Here,
other beings who have chosen to do so, assist newcomers in
understanding the life-and-death process. There are no
secrets in the holding tank, so every question a newcomer has
is addressed openly and honestly.

The assistants are very personable and adept at sensing the personality and needs of each newcomer. They use a variety of techniques to help the newcomers feel welcome and comfortable. They can be humorous, matter-of-fact, gentle, strong, serious, or jovial in attending to the needs of each individual. Jesus Christ also walks in this companion dimension of the Earth, spending time with EVERY newcomer and helping him or her understand how to function fully within these new vibrations.

What form do human beings assume on the other side of life? Obviously, they no longer have a corporeal body. What they do have is an ESSENCE that distinguishes them from others and makes them unique and recognizable to others. That essence is composed of pure energy. It is the immortal half of the human being that never tastes death. It is the life force.

The life force can assume any form he or she chooses. Quite often that is the most recent human form, because this form is what the life force is most comfortable with and represents his or her most significant success. Whatever the choice, these forms are always pleasing. As Dick says, "The body reigns on Earth, but spirit is king of the after-world."

With the help of their assigned guides (assistants), every newcomer does a life review. The purpose of this review is to assess what was done or not done to further perfect knowledge and integrity. THERE IS NO JUDGMENT. The life review is only a process of furthering one's knowledge. In Dick's words, "The Creator does not deal in sin .. only men do."

People who commit suicide are not judged harshly as many think. They return to Earth until they get IT right. "It" means living within integrity by valuing one's self and honoring one's life plan to completion. Those individuals who are damaged on Earth, and as a consequence cannot love, will not be judged either. They will also be treated with great love and afforded the opportunity to objectively assess their earthly journey.

Based upon this personal assessment of strengths and weaknesses each life force determines what he or she will do next. That includes selecting the dimension of consciousness that most closely correlates to the QUALITY OF LIFE he or she has attained *and* what he or she wants to learn. (Quality of life refers to internal stamina and coping skills. Lessons are determined by the ability of the life force to deal with them.)

There are as many options as there are life forces. Reincarnation on Earth and assisting in the holding tank are just two of the multitude of opportunities and dimensions to choose from. Some choose to study under masters; some serve as messengers or helpers, i.e., guides or angels; some go to different planets and galaxies; some even assume forms very different from their prior Earth form. Because the Universe is extensive, so are the choices.

Newcomers do not live in the past. They quickly get on with their new existence. Therefore, they don't often communicate with loved ones left behind. In addition, communication between those living on Earth and those living beyond Earth is possible, but it is not probable. This is because most humans do not have the ability to talk with those who have experienced death. Moreover, part of life is actually dealing with death. This requires separation from our deceased loved ones. Dealing with death helps us appreciate the value of life.

Our family members and friends who have already experienced physical death are not always there to greet us as we pass from life through the PORTAL OF DEATH. This is not perceived as a loss or disappointment because EVERYONE becomes part of our family when we make the transfer to life-after-death. We understand that the members of our Earth family who have preceded us have gone on to other experiences in their quest for perfect knowledge and integrity. This is comfort enough.

Because of the similarities in values and ideas developed with the members of our Earth family, the opportunity is provided to reincarnate with loved ones and go to the same dimensions after death. Loved ones may also form a pact with one another to work together towards perfect knowledge and integrity. Those individuals who do not continue on with loved ones will not suffer loneliness as a result of their individuation. They have the same opportunity for joy, peace, and growth as life forces who progress as a unit.

On Earth, sex is for the purpose of reproduction and to assist people in bonding. It is also for pleasure, but is often abused. What matters in the spirit world is how the life forces treat one another and how much they love. There, life forces bond through emotional and mental intimacy. Intimacy is a joining of ethereal bodies -- an actual BECOMING of the "other." It does not include physical intercourse, but a sharing of energy and light. "It is splendid," according to Dick.

There is a culmination to the life-and-death process when a life force attains pure knowledge and integrity within our Universe. The Earth, also called Gaia, is a life force who attained this state. Gaia then chose to become a planet on which other life forces could work their way to pure knowledge and integrity. Another name for the Earth is ENCHANTMENT because it is a place for miracles small and large . . . a place where we can learn to perform our own miracles.

Where did this cycle of life-and-death start? Beginning and end are mortal concepts and inadequate to the magnitude of existence. Each of us will understand, when we are more capable of doing so, after our stay on Earth. For now it is enough to know that death is not a frightening experience. It is a relief. It is exciting. It is natural and welcome. There is no reason to be sad. Think of death as graduating and going on to bigger and better things and OPPORTUNITIES.

MEDIUM COMMUNICATION WITH DIANA, "THE PEOPLE'S PRINCESS" OF WALES

September 26, 1997

JAN: Diana is joining us with a smile on her face and a tear in her eye.

Q. Diana, what was the purpose of your last existence on the Earth?

I thought maybe you were going to ask me what my last PURCHASE was on the face of the Earth — as all of the paparazzi would want to know (laughing).

At the time that I was on the Earth, I really didn't know what my purpose was. I didn't have a clear sense of myself. I went from day to day, pushed and tugged, and many times was not clear. I wish I had known myself better. I wish I had known the answer to that question when I was on the Earth. But I'm proud to be able to share it with you now.

I contracted, so to speak, with the government of the

Universe to come to the Earth at this time and usher in a new sense of thinking, a new sense of being . . . connected to the heart, connected to the life force, connected to all of the intrinsic things that are so little seen.

It seemed that I wanted a lot when I was there. But I really wanted very little. I only wanted to be loved by my husband and my family and accepted by the members of his family. I discovered in the process of getting and losing the things that I thought meant the most to me that I connected more to myself and to the things that were REALLY important to me. I probably would not have done that had it not been for the pressures in my life, for the challenges in my life, and for the fact that the eye of the world was on me. I see now that the eye of the Universe was on me, too.

It was through the hardships that I came to know myself and what was important to me. That gave me the strength to do what I needed to do. In a way, I didn't know myself at all until I was put in the position to be with the PEOPLE. When I was out there with the people, I felt real. That's when I felt I was me. I never felt that the fame or the notoriety was me. I never felt connected to myself when I had to defend myself to a world in front of TV screens and on radios.

Through my challenges and my suffering, my heart opened. That took me outside of myself and into the entire world. I learned about people who had nothing, and I realized that we all needed to start sharing ourselves with other people. I think it was learning about this concept of sharing — sharing the things that matter the most with one another — that taught me even if I couldn't feed everybody and hold everybody's hand, I could still LOVE everybody. In learning that lesson, I was able to perform my purpose for being on Earth.

In this very round-about way, I took you on a journey into my soul. To answer your question in just a few words — my purpose there was to REMIND PEOPLE TO CARE.

Q. We're from a Starseed group, and we were wondering if you were also a Starseed. If so, what planet or where in the Universe are you from?

That's been a revelation. I left a world in which I felt like a person without a country. Upon my death, I went into a Universe with multitudes of philosophies stemming from multitudes of planets and star systems, each one with its own flavor and culture.

I thought that living up to the expectations of the British was difficult. But now, I look out there and I see a highly populated Universe with as many differences as there were on Earth magnified a million times. This is where it all came back together for me. This is where the sense of it all came to me. Upon leaving the Earth plane and walking into this myriad of existences — a hundred million "countries" — I saw how little I really had suffered.

I would consider myself a Starseed. I came to the Earth with an incredible purpose in the TRANSITION into the fourth dimension. I felt so honored to be asked to do that. Where is my planet of origin? My planet of origin was Andromeda. The place that I came from directly before I entered into the Earth plane, however, was from "The Command." (See "The Command" in the Cosmic Dictionary.)

I worked with The Command in many capacities. One of the capacities that I enjoyed the most was as a botanist aboard their mother ship. I loved the flowers. I loved the trees. I loved the way things grew and flourished. In this environment, I was able to share the incredible love that I had with all of these entities who thrived on love and attention. Though I did many things aboard the ship — I also worked in several administrative capacities — it was my connection to this botanical field that drew the leaders of The Command to ask me to do what I did upon the Earth.

It was the love that I shared with these beautiful, gentle plant creatures — and the opportunity that gave ME to grow in love, and nurturing, and caring — that brought me to the point where The Command felt I could accomplish what I needed to accomplish. They knew that I would literally be going against a Head of State to exemplify caring, love, nurturing, and concern . . . and then carry that outside of my own country and into an entire world.

I had spent time upon the Earth in a few prior incarnations. I did this, primarily, to get use to the vibrations and become aware of what the Earth was about — but not enough to be what you would call "street smart." The people would not have bonded to me if I had been street smart. The Royals are beautiful people, but they're street smart. The people of Britain, the people of Earth, just wanted someone to be SINCERE.

Q. What was the purpose of your dying at such a young age?

Had I lived out my existence longer, many things would have been lost or forgotten over time. The things that I stood for the most were the things that I had been accomplishing most recently.

It's a funny thing that death brings us home. Not only did it bring me home to here, but it brought the people home to what I was doing there. It made my message more obvious, because I died at what you would call an "unseemly" age. If I had died when aged, my story would not have had the impact that it did.

Q. Did you plan your life and death before you came to Earth?

I was partially responsible for some of the decisions that were made about how things would happen within my life. That "position," so to speak, was created by the leaders of The Command. They knew that something needed to be done to touch the hearts of a world and open them up — so people would start caring for one another again and the violence would diminish.

I was "somewhat interviewed" for the position, although they had already pretty well determined it would be me. I was interviewed for the position so I could decide if I felt that I was up to it. At the point that I made that decision, I was able to participate in preparation of some of the particulars of the things that happened within my lifetime.

Q. There were a lot of important people in your life. Would you share something about your relationships with them?

♦ *Charles, your husband*

Charles, dear Charles . . . so unsuited to his family. Had he been brought up in a different family, you would have seen an incredibly sensitive, loving man. He was trained like a dog to fetch, and heel, and run. I remember now the entity that he really is. Don't underestimate his potential. It was necessary that he be the antagonist in my life, in this play that transpired. And he did the job beautifully. He was trained to do the job beautifully. And I honor him for his arrogance, his coldness, his dishonesty, and his deceit with me . . . for it allowed this play to be carried out at much great suffering to himself.

◆   *Queen Elizabeth*

Oh, mother. I wish I could have called her that. I wanted to so many times. I missed having a mother, and I felt it a real quirk of fate that I should end up with a mother so incapable of nurturing an individual, yet so absolutely exquisite in handling a country. The dichotomy in her brought out the best in me — at first the worst, but ultimately the best in me. And I thank her for that.

◆   *Your children, William and Harry*

(Tearfully) It's hard, yet, to talk about them and not miss them beyond everything that words can express.

Wills will carry on my legacy. After a brief bout of learning to be a man, his tenderness and his caring will come through. I worry about Wills because he holds things in. I hope for his sake that he can spend time with my brother, so he can have a chance to express himself and work through his grief. He will make a noble king. He is one of the greatest reasons that I was there — he is to carry a culture into a new dimension — and to do it fabulously!

Harry, sensitive and loving, a mind like a steel trap, a heart as big as gold, will be more challenged. My death will affect him in some difficult ways. He will, seemingly, have more to work through because he is more obvious — and will be more obvious in his experiences to the public. Harry is to show the people how possible it is to be Royal and still be REAL.

♦   *Your brother and sisters*

It was really the difficulties in our lives, with mother leaving, the loss of father, our own individual heartaches, anguish, and grief, that brought us together. We all learned to appreciate each other in the eye of the hurricane. My brother and I seemed to have more opportunities to talk and to share. He became my staff, particularly after father died. He was the one who gave me courage. He was the one who gave me strength. He was the one who lit the fire under me to fight and to make it through. They all played an important part in my life. Even the absences in my life, the times when they weren't there, played an important part in my life and in helping me to understand the things that were really important.

♦   *Your father and mother*

Father was very busy, and yet he did seem to find time for us. I remember as a little girl, father telling us stories and how I loved to listen to him. I thought he must be the grandest person on the face of the Earth. I always felt in some ways cheated that mother didn't live with us, but father did a very good job of trying to fill that gap. I was never left to feel as though I was unworthy because I was "abandoned" by my mother. Actually, mother and I became much closer as I got older. Then I could begin to see what she was all about, and that's when I began forgiving her for leaving us. She taught me a lot. She taught me about integrity, and father taught me about strength. I love them both very dearly.

♦   *Dodi El-Fayed*

It's somewhat hard to talk about that. Dodi had a way of helping me feel fulfilled. He adored me and I knew it. He adored me and I needed it. He adored me and it helped me forget I was a princess and remember I was a person.

We tried to overlook it, but we always knew that the differences in our backgrounds could be a problem — a problem between a woman raised to honor the religion of her own country and a man with, what the world would have seen to be, an improper match with his own religion . . . his religion being not only a religion, but a culture and a way of life.

When we decided that we cared about one another, we chose not to let other people's attitudes and opinions make any difference in our relationship. We also decided that if we chose to continue the relationship — regardless of the type of pressure or criticism that we would get for bringing these two seemingly opposing lifestyles and philosophies together — we were determined to show the world that differences are OK. He gave me the opportunity to do that.

He was a precious, loving man who had to learn to honor himself because he was not treated with honor for a great deal of his life. Yet, he was much stronger than people gave him credit for. He understood life because of his own challenges and difficulties. We could relate to each other on that level.

Q. I'm sure you're aware that there were billions of people watching your incredible funeral. What was your impression of this extraordinary event?

(Laughing) You're assuming I observed the funeral. Parts of it are something of a blur. I was going through my own adjustment at that time into the different vibrations here.

I was rather uncomfortable with the notoriety. Actually, I was shocked. I had no idea that I had made this type of impact. I always felt like a "small town" girl. I never, ever felt special. I felt different. And yet, I know it was necessary that the notoriety be there in order for the message to come through. And I'm glad it came through with respect and honor, and that there was peace in all of it.

The part I watched, the part that had the most significance to me, (tearfully) was watching my two sons walk behind me with courage and dignity — and I knew I had raised TWO KINGS. That is what it was all about for me. That was the most important part.

Q. What did you think of the song Elton John sang for you?

As usual, he was exquisite. I would not have expected less from him — a master, a genius, and still so real. It was a tribute that shall be with me always. It meant even more to me because he's such a wonderful friend.

Q. Is there a message you would like to give to your family now living?

That I'm well. That I'm alive (laughing). That I'm not just a myth of their imagination. I'm not just a ghost. I will be a presence in their lives. I really haven't left.

I am told that I'm going to have the opportunity to

participate in many things — not in human manifest form — but, through my ethereal body, I will again touch the Earth and, hopefully, play a part in many things that come to be. Particularly, as I see my children take their place in this and as the TRANSITION into the higher dimension takes place, I will be participating. Though I won't be seen with the naked eye, I will be there.

Q. Is there a message you would like to leave with us here in this Starseed group?

Yes. Never give up! All of you have missions that you agreed to, that you volunteered for, that you helped plan before you arrived. Don't let sparks of human indignity, ignorance, lack of enlightenment, or lack of graciousness stop you. Don't succumb to anger — supersede it. Make it work for you. Make it show you how to make a success out of what the world would call failure or mistakes.

Don't accept anybody else's explanation of your life. Determine that yourself. Be open to the counsel of the entities around you that you cannot see, but who watch over you and have a vested interest in your success and the success of your missions.

Always hold your heads up high — with humility AND with pride. Don't give in to arrogance. Don't give in to indignity.

Don't give in to wrong-doing. Understand that you have all of the strength that's needed to succeed. Never underestimate yourself. And don't let the viewpoints of the world stop you from succeeding.

Diana, thank you for your life and for sharing your incredible love and strength with us. Many of us miss your extraordinary energy and ask for your help in grieving the loss of your physical presence here on Earth. Please call upon us at any time, so that we can assist the Universe in its plans of love and light.

Thank you. That's a wonderful eulogy. You're getting a round of applause from here. Thank you for the opportunity to let me speak.

Diana

WHY ME?

In 1990, I realized that if I was going to have a peaceful co-existence with my memories, I needed to do something drastic.

On the heels of my soul exchange with Cassy, I had changed jobs. My goal was to further the career path I inherited from her *for* her. I could not step onto my own path until I traveled hers, fulfilling some of her dreams and aspirations . . . those we had agreed upon before our soul exchange took place.

This was not a simple task. I was still learning to walk and talk the "way of the human" and mend a body with a chronic disease. Nevertheless, I took my army of ethereal entities with me to a new arena in corporate America and worked my way up to management. That pleased Cassy a lot. But the Universe didn't let me spin my wheels there for long.

Within a few years, synchronicity dropped me on the doorstep of academia. Cassy's dream of completing her education was behind those doors. So I left corporate America in 1990 and became a full-time student, along with being a full-time single mother of two teenagers. Now those were learning years!

My undergraduate studies in Communication and Journalism took two years to complete and didn't prove to be overly challenging. In fact it was quite fun. I began my graduate program with the same expectation. Was I in for a surprise!

One semester into my Master's course work, Zachary and Uncle Dick entered my life. I soon forgot the meanings of the words "sleep" and "personal life." To my courses in Human Resource Development and Management, I added a new line of instruction in Cosmic Existence — the history, law, sociology, physiology, philosophy, and psychology of the Universe. A year later, I had an unexplainable urge to earn my certification as a Professional Mediator. So I added course work in mediation to my already over-booked project list.

On a rare occasion when I was catching my breath, I realized that I had become so immersed in everything I was learning in Earth School and Cosmic School that I had overlooked something very important. I didn't have a clue WHY Zachary was tutoring ME! What in heaven's name, qualified ME for this course in Cosmic Existence? I hadn't even applied for admission to the Cosmic University. At least, I didn't REMEMBER doing that.

As obvious as it may have seemed to somebody else to have asked that question earlier, it didn't occur to me until 1995 — almost two years after Zachary began tutoring me.

By this time, I knew I wasn't going to be walking a charted course. My feet were planted on the Earth, but my heart, mind, and soul belonged to the Universe. My arrival on the Earth seven years earlier hadn't been ordinary. I was beginning to suspect my future wasn't going to be ordinary either. But what was my future to be, and why had Zachary become my constant companion and mentor? What was my purpose for being here? Why was my life so different from other people's lives?

When I asked Zachary, his first response was to laugh. (While Zachary is the epitome of dignity, he has an extraordinary sense of humor.) "Think back to five years ago," he said, "back to something your teacher, Sharon, told you. You think that your becoming a professional mediator was an accident. Think back."

I did think back. A timer went off in my mind. One of my spiritual teachers, Sharon, had channeled some information to me five years ago. What was it? Now, I remembered. I had forgotten because it didn't seem relevant at the time.

"You are going to teach people how to solve their problems peacefully," she had said to me. I remembered the words verbatim. Bingo! Mediation!

As I mentioned earlier, during the last year of my graduate work I had an unexplainable urge to get my mediation certification. I had contacted the ONE organization in town that gave an introductory mediation class to get on the waiting list for their next class. I had already been advised by somebody else that the next class would not be for another six months. As synchronicity would have it, however, their twice-a-year class started that very night.

That class brought extraordinary meaning into my life. The simplicity and the success of the mediation process fueled my desire to help people learn to deal with conflict in a positive way. I took every training class available in town in the next nine months. Then I traveled to another city and another state to take classes. I got my professional certification and became involved in the Mediation Department in the local District Court.

"But what has this got to do with why you're here with me," I asked Zachary. His response took my breath away.

"There has been a genetic aberration in humans that has caused a propensity for escalated violence. That is why so many of your youth have turned to acts of violence — to satisfy their need for increased sensory stimulation." His next words walked me into the world of government subterfuge and coverups. "Your government has also been conducting genetic research to create perfect warriors. This, too, is creating a propensity for escalated violence amongst your human population."

"But what can I possibly do about this," I demanded to know. "I am one person, and I cannot take on an entire government or an entire population. Besides, who would believe me?"

"You are underestimating your power and the power of other individuals. EVERY time one of you resolves a problem peacefully, the higher vibrations from that success lift the level of consciousness of the planet as a whole. This helps reduce the level of violence on the planet. You now have the ability to teach people how to resolve their problems peacefully. Go and do that."

I have learned that universal law dictates that there will be no direct interference with any planet's system of existence, unless that system seriously jeopardizes the well-being of the rest of the Universe. If we choose to annihilate our human race through our violence, the Universe will not interfere with that decision.

But the Spiritual Forces of the Universe know that the Earth and its inhabitants are in their infancy. They wouldn't abandon us any more than nurturing parents would abandon their children. So, they help us indirectly. They help us by raising our individual and collective consciousness. They help us by sending us teachers like Zachary and Uncle Dick. They reach out with their ethereal hands to guide us, protect us, and console us. And I've learned from personal experience that they do it out of pure love.

Now I had my answer to WHY I was getting a course in Cosmic Existence. I was ready to settle into a comfortable little career as a Professional Mediator. If wishes were horses, my humanness would have been riding Pegasus. Within short order, however, I found myself afoot. And I had only taken my FIRST step onto my cosmic path.

If I had used some foresight here, I would have added some foot remedies to my backpack and saved myself some callouses. My human brain didn't get it yet. But my life force knew it was time to get moving . . . to be about doing what I was here to do. I started referring to this elusive, nebulous accomplishment beckoning to me as my MISSION.

CHANNELING

Jesus Christ: His Autobiography in His Own Words

JAN: When Zachary and I got to the portal to the eighth dimension, Ezekiel and Sananda were waiting outside for us. We all hugged, exchanged greetings, and then went inside. I felt so overwhelmed when I walked in that I almost wanted to back out. There were so many entities present. There are thousands of entities with us now, and we're all ready to begin.

Q. Dearly beloved Sananda, we are in the holiday season on the Earth known as Christmas. We are celebrating the birth of Jesus the Christ of Nazareth. It is our understanding that you were that person who walked upon the Earth almost two thousand years ago. Is this so?

Indeed. I spent a few years there — in your time frame, thirty-some. They were delightful years during which I had the opportunity to commune with many beautiful entities — human, Starseed, and ethereal. During that time, I discovered my mission and who I was, as many of you have. I experienced the best of times and the worst of times. In either case, it was a blessing and a joy that I was able to be there at that time to accomplish what I was sent to accomplish.

Q. Is Sananda the name you prefer to be called? If not, what name do you prefer?

Many of you have connected with your own cosmic names. These names are important because they vibrate to the sound and the level of your own unique life force.

My cosmic father gave me the name, Sananda. I remember my father and my mother at the time that they bestowed this name upon me. They told me the value of my name, that it had been chosen for me, and that it resonated with my mission.

Q. Would you please tell us about your cosmic parents and which dimension and planet or star system you call home?

I have called many planets and star systems home, for my life force has existed in many times and PURPOSES. I have had many cosmic families. I will tell you of my most recent one — the one that prepared me to come to the Earth.

My father is a man of keen insight and judgment, a man

whose integrity was not surpassed anywhere within our Universe. His foresight saw that the Earth and its solar system was going to have great impact upon the Universe. He asked to be a part of that impact. It was my father who created the plan for the Earth to TRANSITION from the second to the third dimension of consciousness two thousand years ago. It was he who asked me to be a part of this plan and gifted me with that mission.

My mother is what you would call "the power behind the throne." She has both tremendous strength and softness. She is an extraordinary example in my life, as my father is. I was blessed beyond comprehension with these two that you would call my parents, my guardians, my teachers.

In this Universe that we now know, there are eight dimensions of consciousness, of existence. When I came to the Earth two thousand years ago, I came from the seventh dimension. Accomplishing my mission upon the Earth at that time was part of my preparation to move into the eighth dimensional consciousness.

The time will come when the doorway will open for you into other Universes — just as your Earth is opening up into THIS Universe through your TRANSITION into the fourth dimension of consciousness. There are many who travel now between the Universes. In those Universes, there are other dimensions of existence.

Q. What was your mission in coming to the Earth two thousand years ago?

My life was quite well known, but my mission was misunderstood in many ways. Many thought that because I had the capability of raising the dead, of healing, and performing what they called miracles, that I must be a god. Your gods, my beloveds, came from what you call "out there," and there are multitudes of them. If you want to look at it that way, then indeed, I am ONE of your gods.

But you choose to believe that "God" is that one singular entity who is all powerful and all knowing. So, I would introduce you to that power known as "The Creator." It was with the approval of The Creator and in conjunction with The Creator, that my beloved father and mother prepared this journey for me.

My journey here to the Earth was only to bring enlightenment — enlightenment such as those beautiful entities Princess Diana and Sister Theresa inspired in you. My mission was as theirs — to raise consciousness by bringing higher vibrations to the Earth. With my vibrations, I brought understanding, knowledge, and words that could help people lift themselves out of their ignorance and their destitution to touch the stars.

In coming to Earth, I let people know that they were part

of a bigger concept . . .that they were part of a world that knew goodness and peace . . . a world that knew a consciousness that allowed people to work together for the same beautiful ends.

I came to show people that this is not a world of tit-for-tat. So, I brought ACCEPTANCE with me. With that, I was able to raise the vibrations of the Earth. I didn't do this alone. I did it in conjunction with many others who were upon the face of the Earth at that time. Together — even though we were separated by many, many miles — our singular vibrations joined to raise the collective vibrations of the Earth from the second to the third dimensional level of consciousness.

Q. Did you take part in the decisions involving your mission?

I certainly had the opportunity to accept or reject this beautiful plan that had been prepared for me. As you will remember from your readings in your Bible, there was a time when I knew that the nails were soon to be thrust into my hands. I did not want the pain, and I did not want the agony. But never did I not want to fulfill my mission. So, despite the pain that I knew I would suffer, I forged ahead with strong conviction. I had disquiet inside myself, knowing that my flesh and bones would suffer the pain of the cross. But never did I doubt that I would complete this beautiful, beautiful plan that had been prepared for the Earth.

Q. Would you please tell us about your conception and the belief that yours was a virgin birth.

An interesting concept, is it not? Remember, anything is possible in existence . . . anything. A reality is only limited by our own thoughts, by our own beliefs.

In fact, that blessed woman upon the Earth who served as my human mother was "taken up." She was taken up into the cosmos, where she had a blessed and sacred union with my father. In this way, the seed was prepared for my life force — a virgin birth — a union between a mortal, corporeal woman and an immortal, ethereal man.

Q. Would you please share with us the circumstances surrounding your birth?

The thing that I remember most about entering the Earth realm was the feeling that I got from my beloved human mother. I felt the love that poured out of her for me and for the man who served as my human father. I remember how HE stood there in all confidence and strength to protect and support the two of us.

I remember that I could see the animals around me. The

feeling of love that I felt for and from these animals was extraordinary. This was an unusual phenomenon, as children do not usually see or feel so clearly at birth. Because everything was so clear and so pristine to me, I felt like I had entered an infant body as a grown man.

I remember that there were other entities present that only my mother, my father, and I could see. The room seemed filled with ethereal bodies. They gave me much encouragement, much love. The angel energies were present amongst these. There were also those who were there to watch over me, protect me, and guide me throughout my life. Many of these stayed with me through the duration of my Earth existence. It was a time of beauty, a time of rest.

To the others present, my birth must have seemed quite innocuous. For they would not have known nor felt the presence of the ethereals as we did. But for the three of us, it was a glorious experience.

Q. So there were, indeed, angels present?

Yes. The angel energies are such beautiful energies. They are so loving, so nurturing, so protective. They were there from the very beginning of my existence and to the very end.

Q. Who are the three "wise men" we have heard about, and can you explain the star they followed to find you?

That is a very interesting story. The "wise men" were those you would call Starseed. Some time before my birth, they were told that I would be arriving on Earth and that it was intended for them to spend time with me. They were told to follow "the star." The star that brought them to me was their own internal "guiding lights."

These very wise men did not arrive at the time of my birth. But, more appropriately, they manifested individually within the first three years of my life. We actually spent time talking to one another. Does it seem strange that such a small child could talk to three adult Starseed?

When they came to me, I was able to tell these Starseed of my mission and my purpose — which was part of their mission and their purpose. With this information, they went back out into the world to help enlighten others — to teach others the consciousness of ACCEPTANCE.

Q. We have heard that your life force was so expansive that your body could not contain it and you floated above your sleeping place. If that is so, how was this circumstance resolved?

It has been said that this was so. I don't remember

floating above my sleeping place, but I do remember looking out and seeing my life force so expansive that it lit the entire room. It was not necessary to balance that phenomenon; it was only a blessing to enjoy it.

Q. Please tell us about those parts of your life on Earth that are most appropriate for us to know at this time.

The most appropriate thing for you to know at this time is that all of you should have mastered this principle of ACCEPTANCE in your life — knowing that it is possible to have different attitudes, different values, different feelings, and still ACCEPT one another.

As the fourth dimensional consciousness opens up and you have the opportunity to walk through that portal, this Principle of Acceptance is the most important thing for you to know. For, that period of your third dimensional consciousness is at an end. Coming in upon your shoulders are all of your oversouls — those parts of you who have been living in other dimensions and other times, and who have been learning, just as you have been. You are all coming together to create that whole beautiful you again . . . to understand that your feet no longer must stay and walk upon the Earth . . . to know that you may now walk into the Universe and upon the stars.

Q. Have you or any of your oversouls had other incarnations upon the Earth?

I have had many oversouls who have had incarnations upon the Earth. My oversouls have manifested in many different forms — the beggar woman, the peasant man, the homeless man upon the street, the teacher, the policeman, the political leader, the student. I have also had oversouls manifest as Krishna and the Buddha. That entity you knew as Mahatma Gandhi was a very dear, beloved friend and oversoul of mine.

My own feet have not walked again upon the Earth since that time they left almost two thousand years ago. However, I have been represented upon the Earth many times through my oversouls.

Q. What activities and purpose are you now involved in?

From the time of my inception into this plan to bring enlightenment and higher dimensional consciousness to the Earth, the Earth has been my focus. Though I do travel to other places, to other dimensions, and into other galaxies and other Universes as I choose, my primary focus has been in care and guardianship of the Earth.

Q. Where does one go when one transcends the highest dimension in our Universe? Where will you go?

That is the choice of the individual entity. Most entities choose to step out into the other Universes to experience new and different things. They may also choose to stay in this Universe. I have not yet made that decision, nor will I make that decision until after the Earth has transitioned into the fourth dimensional consciousness. I suspect that I will stay here in this Universe a while longer. At some time, however, it will be appropriate for me to join my father in another Universe.

Q. Will you be returning to the Earth at any time? If so, when, for what purpose, and what will be the circumstances surrounding your return?

What you call the TRANSITION is when I will come again. I will come to welcome you to the fourth dimension of consciousness and allow you to say goodbye to the dimension of consciousness that I brought you. It is a time for goodbyes and welcomes, and I will be there with you to participate in this. Many others will come with me. Our arrival will be known and noted, and we will help you with this TRANSITION.

I have brothers and sisters upon the Earth now, preparing in conjunction with my own oversouls for what will be transpiring shortly upon your Earth. They are preparing themselves to prepare others for your TRANSITION into the fourth dimensional consciousness. I have a younger brother who will be manifesting upon the Earth at the time of this TRANSITION. He will stand before you in youth form to assist your youth in their TRANSITION.

Q. What can we, the Starseed, do to prepare for your return?

You are already transitioning into the next dimension of consciousness. Continue what you are doing — learning to live ACCEPTANCE . . . learning to remember those higher dimensions of consciousness that you came from, where there was a greater capacity for love, sensitivity, compassion, kindness, giving, and sharing . . . learning to remember your strength and your power . . . remembering who you are.

It is important that you work very hard every single day to remember what your missions are. Do this so that when the most challenging part of this TRANSITION is upon you, you will work with confidence and in unison with one another.

Develop with us, your brothers and sisters in the sky, the ability to communicate. Get to know us. Let go of your fear of us. Reach out to us and start talking to us so we may guide you through this TRANSITION. Let us be there to help you; after all, you are helping us.

You have taken upon yourselves the heaviness of the human body and the pain of violence and misunderstanding to fulfill your missions. We honor you for this. We thank you for this. We ask you to let us be a part of helping you. Your key to this is ACCEPTANCE . . . acceptance of those who are different from you upon the EARTH . . . and acceptance of those who are different from you in the rest of the UNIVERSE.

Q. Is there anything else that is appropriate for us to know at this time?

The most important thing for you to remember is that we love you with all of our hearts. There are millions of us who look upon you and honor what you do. We encourage you. We are your cheerleading section. We are your guides and your angels. You are never alone. Our hearts, our thoughts, and our actions are with you in everything that you do.

Sananda

Q. Zachary and Ezekiel, is there anything you would like to add that would assist us in enjoying a personal relationship with Sananda the Christ?

We wish only to say that it is our divine blessing to work with an entity who has so extraordinarily fulfilled his mission and serves as a light to all of the Universe.

We see Sananda in all of his love. We also see him in all of his humor. There are many sides and facets to this entity you once called Jesus the Christ. He can be fun. He can be pensive. He can be quiet. He can be loud. He can be firm. He can be gentle. In all of his aspects, we are proud to call him brother and friend.

Zachary & Ezekiel

MY TURN

The Transcendents have no clocks. Our communications can take place when I'm in the shower, while I'm on the phone, and even while I'm walking down a crowded street. On this particular day in August of 1995, Zachary's message came to me while I was sunbathing in the back yard. The circumstances seem innocuous in comparison to the message. My life changed forever in those few moments.

"Your real name is Janis. You spell it J-A-N-I-S," Zachary told me. "You have completed your work for Cassy. Now it is your turn. It is time to do your own mission."

I had spent the last eight years resolving Cassy's relationships, completing her education, and raising our children. Now I was to do my thing. But, WHAT was my thing?

Prompted by Zachary, I left for Aspen, Colorado, three days later. The ten days I spent there were magical. I had never been to Aspen, and I knew no one there when I arrived. When I left, however, I was rich in friendships and memories.

I stayed at a charming bed and breakfast while I was there. Over breakfast, we philosophized about life, death, God, and What Really Is. I found that people were more hungry for spiritual nourishment than for fruit and cereal. I was asked to do a group channeling which turned into six hours of intimate sharing between strangers. Bonds of enlightenment and appreciation were formed. Differences disappeared as all present lovingly shared their own insights. I let go of my own fear of sharing myself and my spiritual abilities.

I delivered my message and concluded my stay with a mystical day at the top of Aspen Mountain with a friend. Zachary and I talked, and he gifted me with the photograph of him that you will find on the first page of this book. The vibrations on the mountain were joyous and spoke peace to our hearts. It is a day I shall always cherish.

When I returned home, I was no longer afraid to talk about my beliefs, experiences, and spiritual abilities. I had stepped onto the Transcendent Highway. Since then, I've gone many miles. I've slowed down, sped up, changed lanes, and even had an accident or two. I've met many beautiful people along the way. Some were monied. Some were homeless. To me, they were all rich.

"I can't see,"
said the boy as he looked into the sun.

"That is because, 'Greedy One,'
you want to see it all at once.
You're not using good judgment."

"Look, instead, at the bird in the sky.

It is free because it demands so little.
And it is joyful because it is free."

"So, go and make no demands on others;
walk softly upon the Earth;
and live simply.
Be free and be joyful."

Zachary

I feel rich. I've taken a road few others have traveled and thereby found myself. Amazingly, the accounts of my spiritual adventures have been welcomed — even sought out — by others. Every time I've seen my words spark a glow of remembrance in THEIR eyes, it has strengthened MY determination to forge on . . . on with my own remembering and my mission . . . ordinary or not.

CHANNELING

We're Not Here to be Ordinary

JAN: Zachary has brought me to the top of a mountain. We are going to do our channeling here, at the top of this mountain.

There is another entity with Zachary, Ezekiel, Sananda, and myself. This entity is difficult to describe. He is what I would envision or think of in terms of vibrations as an incredible guru. They say he is a teacher who lives now upon the Earth. He is so advanced that he has always had to exist apart from the every day third dimensional things that transpire.

This teacher is here to address questions that involve an understanding of third dimensional Earth activities. He will share with us how we can transcend and stay beyond the grasp of the third dimensional negativity and demands.

"But we walk amongst third dimensional entities every day, live in third dimensional buildings, and eat third dimensional food. How is it possible to transcend third dimensional demands when we are in corporeal form?" I ask him.

"Do you think this is a necessity?" he queries me. "You are not here to be third dimensional. You are here to raise the vibrations of your bodies to the point that you need NOT be a part of the third dimension. You don't need the things of the third dimension. BELIEVE that, and it will be so."

"You need not even walk upon the Earth in corporeal form. You can manifest and look to others as if you are corporeal, but you need not be. There are many who have walked upon the Earth, and even now do so, who are not of the corporeal."

"Don't allow yourself to fall into the complaints, the criticisms, the condemnations — those things you call the 'three C's' — of the third dimension. Rise above them. Rise above their negativity. For, you can."

"Never doubt your ability. Never doubt your power. Let go of limitations. Let go of expectations and judgments of people and things. In doing so is your credibility. Never forget that — in doing so is your credibility."

"You are not here to be ordinary!"

The Mountaintop Guru

FINDING THE STARSEED

Who was I? What was I? Human? I guess so. I had a human body, but my life force had very real, recent, vivid connections with "out there." I knew from my cosmic education with Zachary that I was here to do something different from the norm . . . a MISSION, I called it. But I wasn't sure what it was. I did know it wasn't where I was presently living — but where? I just wasn't getting it.

I really was resistant to change. Seven years earlier I had bought the house in which I raised the children and intended to retire. My human family was nearby. I thought that scenario was all I needed. But the call of the cosmos was stronger, and the winds of change were whipping around me. I knew I had to give up the security of familiarity.

This realization was hard-earned. It came on the heels of a year-and-a-half of turmoil in my life. Losses became the theme that forced me to understand — losses in love, financial security, and trust seemed overwhelming. Betrayal, particularly by two beloved friends, finally forced me out of the nest. At the time, I was hurt and angry beyond comprehension. Now I thank them with my whole heart for playing this part in my life and forcing me to embrace a bigger picture.

"My friend, why on Earth did you bite me?"
asked the man of the fox.

"Because I love you."

"That's ridiculous.
You don't hurt someone you love."

"You told me you wanted to heal the wounds
of the world," replied the fox.
"How can you learn the power of healing
if you have nothing to heal?"

"You make a good point, my sly friend,
and I thank you for your gift
. . . despite the pain I suffer."

Zachary

I did the only thing I could do at the time. I conceded to UNCONVENTIONAL wisdom. I sold almost everything I owned and bought a motor home. I asked Zachary to take me where the Universe wanted me. Then my dog, two cats, and

I hit the road in our new home on wheels.

I had never ridden in a motor home, much less driven one. I had no mechanical aptitude. I did have a goal, though. I was going to spend the rest of my life in spiritual endeavors. It seemed a very small matter that I didn't know exactly how I was going to accomplish that.

Once I made that decision, THE DECISION, I knew it was the appropriate one. I was excited! I was riding on a cloud of anticipation, and I had AAA.

Four tows and five mechanics later, AAA proved to have been a very wise decision. Nevertheless, Las Vegas was the end of the line for the motor home. I had the engine overhauled, but I couldn't bring myself to sit behind the wheel again. Besides, my four-legged "kids" made it clear they would no longer tolerate an engine in their living room. I promised I would get them a new home.

Las Vegas was not my choice to visit for long and certainly was not a place I intended to call home. I immediately began my search for a fifth wheel and truck to get back on the road.

"Not so quick," Zachary whispered in my ear. I pretended I didn't hear.

While I wasn't listening, I found a fifth wheel but no truck. My car wouldn't sell, and it was illegal to pull it behind a fifth wheel. The weather was great, my family came to visit, and I made some wonderful friends. I devised plans to go to Arizona, but my cat got sick. On my second try for Arizona, my son came to visit for five weeks. I couldn't escape! Now what? I was out of money and I was hungry. But what I needed was spiritual food.

The time that I had spent traveling was saturated with long and intense conversations with Zachary. I experienced four days of "lost time." My learning curve was at its peak. By this time, I knew my own origin was Pleiades and that Zachary was not only my teacher and mentor, he was my Pleiadian father. I also knew I was sent here directly from the cosmos to accomplish something specific in terms of helping the Earth and its residents. I also knew I was on the verge of finding out WHAT that something specific was.

I was craving to be with others like myself, but for all I knew I was alone. I didn't consider myself an "abductee" (*see Cosmic Dictionary*). All my experiences with "non-humans" had been very positive and loving. I hoped to find what I called "contactees." Surely there had to be others in contact with benevolent transcendent forces. I went into a meta-physical bookstore to see if I could find a contactee group. No luck, but they offered me a job as a psychic reader. Why not? It was a step forward on my unconventional spiritual path.

DON'T FOLLOW
CONVENTIONAL WISDOM
It puts you in your place.

My goal as a psychic reader was spiritual. The first thing that I had to do was overcome the negative thinking surrounding the word "psychic." I found this term fit a certain caliber of clientele at the store — curiosity hounds; people who wanted short-term fixes to their problems; those wanting the numbers to the lottery; people who wanted to rely on others to make most of their decisions, also known in the business as "psychic junkies;" and even some who wanted to cast spells on other people. I minimized my contact with those playing these games of trivial pursuit.

Less than five percent of the store's clientele even knew what channeling, empathing, or mediumship were. That proved to be an opportunity rather than a problem, however. The serious seekers were comparatively easy to teach. They were drawn to the love, insight, and accuracy behind the information they received from these processes. For those who didn't comprehend the information at the time, the seeds of consciousness were planted for later harvest.

There were some who stood out more than others. They were the fulfillment of my spiritual goal. They were comprised of exotic dancers, businessmen, millionaires, doctors, nurses, retirees, people out of work, cocktail waitresses, teachers, casino workers, homemakers, policemen, military, and many others. They came in every color in the human rainbow. Most of all, they were people searching . . . searching to know themselves in the context of a bigger picture than their everyday survival activities. They were searching for the MEANING in their existence.

Consciousness, simply stated, is

KNOWING ONESELF

. . . as a human being

AND

. . . as a citizen of the Universe

In helping these people better understand themselves (their talents, desires, strengths, personalities, goals, jobs, and relationships), a very surprising pattern emerged. I discovered that many were humanly challenged in an unconventional sense.

These clients felt different and misplaced. Many didn't "fit" into their families, and some even lacked childhood memories. Others felt as though they would never experience death. Most felt appalled at violence, as if they remembered an existence lacking this phenomenon. Many had very little interest in money or possessions, but did have a strong drive to improve the world and the lot of others.

This quest to better the collective standard included a strong sense of having a mission and being on some kind of time table. Surprisingly, many had active clairvoyant abilities of their own and felt a connection to "higher sources." Consistent among all of them, however, was a distinct void of meaning in their current lives, as if they had not connected with themselves and their purpose in this existence.

Another pattern started to emerge, as well. In the channelings, I started receiving information from Zachary that these people were not "human incarnates." That is, they had come from other planets, star systems, and even other galaxies and universes. After a significant number of readings, I discovered that the majority had actually come from the Pleiadian and Sirius star systems. Consistently, they were all referred to in the channelings by Zachary as "Starseed."

Within a short time, these Starseed began referring others to me. A significant number of my readings came to be identifying the Starseed, telling them what planets they were from, what their specific missions were, and the cosmic names they were known by in the Universe.

I started referring the Starseed to a support group for abductees. My hope was that the "ET link" would provide them with information that could help them get a better sense of themselves. This worked in the short run, but it became obvious that the Starseed were also hungry for cosmic instruction — they wanted to learn more in terms of CONSCIOUSNESS.

I quit my job at the bookstore and started focusing on the Starseed. When it became obvious that the abductee group was focused primarily on the fear and emotional issues associated with this phenomenon, I started a Starseed group myself to provide guidance in the area of consciousness.

The speed on the winds of change picked up to hurricane proportions. Fortunately, I was safely in the eye of the hurricane — channeling constantly, asking questions, getting answers, focusing on the needs of the Starseed. So powerful was the information I was receiving, that two other extraordinary ethereal beings joined Zachary to assist in guiding and directing me in my endeavors with the Starseed.

You know one of these beings as Jesus Christ, who came here two thousand years ago to raise the Earth's awareness of the power of love. I call him Sananda. I know him as a dearly beloved brother who raised the consciousness of the Earth from the second dimensional level to the third dimensional level through his energy and teachings on the universal Principle of Acceptance.

The other being who joined this trio is the cosmic brother of Sananda. This being has dedicated himself to the guardianship of the Earth and to preserving the third dimensional consciousness here in honor of his brother's mission. I call him Ezekiel. Some refer to him as Ashtar (see "Ezekiel-Ashtar" in the Cosmic Dictionary for an explanation of the difference in names).

I have learned through the teachings of these magnificent beings and also through my travels into different dimensions, that there are eight dimensions (or levels of consciousness) in our particular Universe. Those beings who have the greatest understanding of the Universe, and whose life forces are of the highest vibration, exist at the eighth dimensional level. Each of these three beings — Zachary, Sananda, and Ezekiel — exist at this eighth dimensional level of consciousness.

I call Zachary, Sananda, and Ezekiel the Transcendents because their consciousness and capabilities transcend that of the third dimensional Earth. Each of these beings is unique and brings to our channelings his own distinct personality and expertise. In an attempt to help you develop an understanding and personal recognition of each of the Transcendents, I have included a brief biographical sketch of each one for you.

To honor the man who welcomed me into existence on Alcyone in the Pleiades and who has nurtured, taught, counseled, and loved me for many hundreds of years, I will start by introducing you to Zachary, my father.

ZACHARY

Because Zachary is of the highest level of consciousness in the Universe, and therefore in the Pleiadian system, he serves on the Pleiadian "Council of Elders." As a leader on the council, he is responsible for the more than 200 planets from five dimensions of consciousness in that star system. Zachary was not elected to this position. It is part of the system of leadership in the Pleiades that those of the highest level of spirituality clearly and naturally assume their position on the Council. It requires a great deal of knowledge, wisdom, diplomacy, and understanding in the ways of the Universe to guide such a large number of planets from so many diverse dimensions.

Zachary is the embodiment of all of these qualities. It is reflected in his appearance, as well. He is quite tall and large of stature. His hair is white and flows over his broad shoulders. It matches his well-groomed beard and the white flowing robe in which he is usually attired. He is the epitome of dignity.

Zachary is the consummate diplomat and the most extraordinary teacher I have ever encountered. He has a way of pointing out my errors in thinking and behavior that makes me eager to change. He calms me in times of stress, helping me to stay focused and in tune with the oh-so-many principles I am constantly recalling here.

To my present knowledge, Zachary has had two incarnations on Earth. One was as Paul (Saul) of Tarsus. This lifetime was very intense and demanding of him, though he established himself as a devoted, beloved, and successful icon of the causes he championed. His other lifetime was in Britain. He tells me it was here that he learned how to relax and enjoy Earth existence. It is from this lifetime and place that he pulls the name "Luv," which he often calls me. He uses this term to remind me that even though I receive information that seems painful or overwhelming at times, I am to deal with it strictly as information and keep my attitude positive and joyful.

Zachary has spent other times on the Earth, though not in corporeal body. One of my fondest recollections was of the time my twin sister, Alcion, and I were allowed to walk the Earth in ethereal form with Zachary and our mother. It was in the ancient Egyptian times. Father and mother were observed as Egyptian gods because they came "from the sky" to visit the Earth. Alcion and I were referred to affectionately, but with much less dignity, as the "god's kids." In Earth time, Alcion and I would have been comparable to about the age of twelve. Though we kept our ethereal forms, the Egyptians could see us clearly and we spent much time laughing and associating with them while father and mother did their "godly" thing.

I remember this time fondly as a time of play and fun. Though young in Earth terms, Alcion and I were highly educated in the ways of the Earth and the Universe. We were, therefore, allowed to assist in the planning of the pyramids. Initially, the pyramids were landing spots for space craft and housed centers of advanced schooling on the Earth. I remember vividly that Alcion and I added a "cubby hole" in the plans of one of the pyramids. We would sit there by the hours and talk of things of the Earth and the Universe (we had done a great deal of traveling throughout the Universe by this time and were considered seasoned travelers). We thought we had really "put one over" on father and mother with this addition to the blueprint. I'm sure Zachary got quite a chuckle out of our harmless divisiveness.

I have many more fond personal memories of Zachary that I will include in a following section on cosmic families. For now, suffice it to say that Zachary is more real and vital to me than most of the associations I have made on Earth in the last eleven years I have been here.

SANANDA

Sananda, because of his association with the Earth two thousand years ago as Jesus Christ, is more familiar to you than any of the other Transcendents. I see him in a much more personal light and much less as a historical figure.

It is always apparent when Sananda speaks in the channelings. Because of his own personal experience as Jesus, his words are filled with love, understanding, and compassion. His love is so boundless that it usually spills over through my eyes.

I have spent much time in conference with Sananda, Zachary and Ezekiel on the mother ship. The mother ship is the Command's base of operations. It is housed in a very large "space station" (for lack of a better word) that is home to millions of extraterrestrials in service to the Earth. These extraterrestrials are from a variety of clans from our own galaxy, other galaxies, and even other universes. Life on the mother ship includes lively operating activities, as well as the personal activities of the unique and varied individuals who reside there.

The four of us usually meet in a conference room with the three Transcendents on one side of a table and I on the other. Sananda always shows much focus and, at times, great concern. But more than anything, there is always his great love and his unconquerable hope. It is perhaps his sincerity and serenity, however, that affect my own viewpoint the most. His example has built inside of me an indomitable trust and dedication to my mission.

I discovered in the Starseed my own mission. At first, I felt it . . . so strongly that the joy of meaningfulness swallowed me into the abdomen of other realities.

Here I stood — in a room at a conference table with Zachary, Sananda, and Ezekiel sitting across from me. I saw my true form — tall, straight, strong, powerful . . . dressed in a blue Pleiadian jump suit . . . honey-red hair falling straight to my elbows . . . eyes fixed and firm. I stated my case for more cosmic assistance for my beloved Starseed.

I knew then that I had been sent to bring the Starseed together under the banner of consciousness and service. I remembered that I was to help them remember their origins and their missions and to help prepare them for their primary purpose in being here at this time — to assist the Earth and the Eartheans in their TRANSITION into the next dimension of higher consciousness.

Janis Abriel

I always feel tremendously at ease and comfortable with Sananda wherever we meet in the other dimensions. When Sananda, Zachary, Ezekiel, and I come together to channel, it is Sananda's smile that integrates my being back into the ethereal vibrations.

It is difficult to describe Sananda's personage. Since his energy is so high and bright, often what I see is simply form and light. At those times when I do see him more distinctly, he has manifested to me in two different forms. In council with the other Transcendents and me, Sananda appears very similar to Zachary — large of stature and dressed in a white robe, with white flowing hair and beard. They tell me that the similarity in their appearance is due to the similarity in their vibrations.

When we are not in council with the other Transcendents, Sananda assumes a more youthful form. Such a time was when Sananda and I walked the mother ship together discussing family. As he spoke of his cosmic parents and siblings, his eyes glowed and his smile was infectious. I felt his admiration in his radiant energy, as well as in his words. It was a delightful interlude of laughing and sharing. In fact, my association with Sananda and his family precipitated some startling conscious remembrances from my own cosmic past which are important to share with you now.

When we get to the dimensions in the Universe that do not require corporeal forms, the nature of our existence changes drastically. These are the realms of the life force independent of a mortal body. As the life force is immortal, there is no birth process, at least not as we know it. Life forces

enter a particular experience or existence for a particular
PURPOSE. The life force may choose to enter the experience in
youthful form or in adult form — whatever best suits the
PURPOSE of the existence.

Both Sananda and his brother, Ezekiel, joined their
family at the request of their father-to-be. Sananda was invited
into this family unit to fulfill this father's plan to raise the
consciousness of the Earth from the second to the third
dimension. Ezekiel was invited into this family unit to fulfill
another critical aspect of this plan — guardianship of the Earth
and its third dimensional consciousness.

EZEKIEL

To introduce you to Ezekiel, I am going to share some
of his own words and explanations with you. Besides giving
you more insight into Ezekiel himself, you will hear more
about the Earth and the nature of your own existence within
the Universe.

---

*It is said that you are Sananda's brother. Would
you verify the accuracy of this?*

This is so. It is very important to understand that the coming into a specific existence
in a higher dimension is not the same as it is on

your Earth. You think of birth in terms of birthing a physical body. In fact, in the ethereal realms FAMILIAL relationships are more a WELCOMING-IN process into a specific purpose. It can happen in a number of ways.

I came into my family — as did Sananda — not as a child. We were both welcomed into the existence in more mature form.

We understand that you are in a guardianship position for the Earth. What is the purpose of this?

I came into this guardianship at the request of my brother, Sananda, when he chose to accept the plan for raising the Earth to the third dimensional consciousness. I was asked if I would not prove to be the guardian of this dimension. So, I have been for the last two thousand years, as you see it.

The other association with your name is "The Command." Would you tell us about The Command and what this name means?

In fact, it's more a situation of our being at the command of the Spiritual Forces of the Universe. If you look at it in those terms — that our services are at the command of the Spiritual Forces to assist in the preservation of consciousness upon the Earth — that is the most important thing to know about the Command.

We are here to ensure that this dimension of your consciousness has been allowed free agency. Your Earth family is truly in its infancy and does not yet know (nor does its solar system) of its relationship to the rest of the Universe. As such, your civilization is not yet competent to preserve the integrity of its third dimensional consciousness.

For this purpose, our service is at the command of the Spiritual Forces — to ensure your protection from other elements that might cause confusion in your world and upset the level of consciousness which you have attained.

Think of this in terms of having an infant child you want to protect. You allow that child to interact with certain things. Other things you protect your child from because your child does not have the level of awareness or consciousness to deal with them.

In what ways do you perform this guardianship? What are your duties?

We ensure that the other clans in the Universe do not interfere with your evolution — societal, physical, as it is — unless there is a universal directive to involve them in some way. Primarily, we're here to preserve that thing you call "free agency," what we call here the "free will Universe."

Consciousness grows at its own pace within each individual and within each dimension. To force the societies outside of your existence onto you would be a huge mistake in the development of your consciousness. Therefore, we watch over you to ensure that you are allowed to proceed at your own pace, and that forces that would not be beneficial to this are not allowed to interfere.

Since you're getting close to completing your TRANSITION into the fourth dimension, we are also working to ensure the well-being of your Earth through this TRANSITION. Through time, we have watched over the physical well-being of the Earth. We have, at times, ensured that the axis of the Earth is preserved. We have ensured that your biosphere was preserved — things of this nature. All of the Starseed who come into your Earth must go through us to ensure that they are spiritually competent to be there, particularly at this time of your TRANSITION.

Ezekiel

As a Starseed with a specific mission of my own here on Earth, my relationship with Ezekiel has been the most difficult to FEEL. After experiencing only sporadic but deeply emotional memories of my cosmic relationship to Ezekiel, the reason for this impasse finally came home to roost in my human brain — my relationship with Ezekiel is perhaps the closest relationship I have in the cosmos. Potentially, my association with Ezekiel threatens my desire to remain on Earth and fulfill my mission here.

Ezekiel and I first met in another Universe. We were brought together in a sibling relationship. To our own amazement, we discovered that we were remarkably similar in vibrations. This manifested in a unison of values, goals, and behaviors. We became, literally, AS ONE.

At the culmination of this experience, I was asked to participate in my most recent Pleiadian experience with Zachary and the rest of my Pleiadian family (detailed later). Part of my purpose in this Pleiadian manifestation was to participate in a plan developed by the Pleiadian Council of Elders in conjunction with the Confederation of Planets and the Spiritual Forces of our Universe. This plan included the pairing of myself and my other Pleiadian brothers and sisters with chosen mates to create spiritually evolved (child) entities with specific vibrational capabilities.

The choice of my particular mate was left to the Council of Elders and the Spiritual Forces. I agreed to abide by their decision. When they announced their choice to me, I was taken completely by surprise. Then my life force resonated with the appropriateness and wisdom of their reasoning. Their choice quickly became my choice — Ezekiel. Ezekiel concurred and our paths bonded once again.

We became companions and parents. When I was called by the Council of Elders to take Cassy's place on Earth, Ezekiel assisted in my preparation. Together we prepared our children for my departure. He was there when my soul exchange was culminated — the companion it was so heart-wrenchingly difficult for me to leave (see chapter on The Exchange).

The veil of my new humanity immediately clouded my remembrance of Ezekiel. Slowly, however, as I have proven my dedication to my mission on Earth, this veil has been lifting. Here is what I can now see.

The first thing I see are Ezekiel's eyes. They're brilliant green like mine — my true eyes, not my human eyes. His form is very tall and slender. The definition in his face — the jaw, the cheeks, the nose — is very angular, very chiseled.

I see Ezekiel's hair as salt- and- pepper. However, he is telling me this is my own perception.

Ezekiel is reminding me that his true form is ethereal. He only takes these manifestations, as do the other ethereals, so there is a sense of connectedness between people.

He says they save their very true ethereal form for contacts with their closest union and relationships.

I see Ezekiel with a smile on his face and a twinkle in his eye. He's saying to me, "I like to keep that twinkle there so people don't forget that when I become focused on fulfilling my responsibilities I still have a sense of humor, and that I'm really a very kind person. What I try to maintain most in what I do is my sense of humor so that the people I work with feel comfortable with me . . . so they don't keep themselves at a distance . . . so they feel that they can approach me."

"It is my extreme desire that people would think of me as a gentle man, as is my brother, Sananda . . . and as a man with a purpose, who garners all of his abilities to accomplish that."

Ezekiel & Janis

Just as Zachary is a teacher of the highest order and Sananda is the epitome of love and compassion, Ezekiel exemplifies distinguished dedication and integrity in fulfilling his own mission to the Earth and The Command.

I have spent a substantial amount of time with Ezekiel since having reconnected with him here in my Earth experience, not only in conjoint channelings with Zachary and Sananda, but also one-on-one. We have talked in great detail. I have also asked him numerous pointed questions and re-experienced our relationship as companions and parents. Now the association I have with Ezekiel is entirely through his ethereal form.

These three unique entities, each with their own specific

personality and strengths, have come to be the backbone of my connection to the Starseed. Just like the spine gives structure to the body and houses the nerve center that directs its operation, so the Transcendents have shaped my relationship with the Starseed and my Earthean brothers and sisters.

Zachary's, Sananda's, and Ezekiel's personalities and awareness resonate like a finely tuned instrument when they are together. My relationship with them is a doorway into a space of pure balance . . . a space where I breathe the pure, clear vibrations of unconditional love.

CHANNELING

Tuning Up Spiritually: Getting & Staying in Balance

Q. As you go from dimension to dimension, does balance shift in its definition?

In all the dimensions, balance results from an understanding of how to use ENERGY. In the eighth dimension, the highest dimension of consciousness within our Universe, there exists a greater ABILITY to control and manipulate energy. This ability is used for the betterment of ALL. You call that "humanity" on your Earth.

So, balance does not shift as much in definition from one dimension to the next as it does in ability.

Balance gives one an ability to experience greater vibrations. It becomes, therefore, an incredible ally. It becomes what one always works and strives for. Balance also becomes easier as you go up through the dimensions. For, as one's dimensional consciousness raises, balance becomes "more at home" within one's life force.

Q. How do those in the eighth dimension handle the balance between thoughts and feelings? In other words, how do they work it out between, say a Mr. Spock (from Star Trek) and a touchy-feely personality? There is merit in both.

How you deal with thoughts and feelings in your dimension is based upon the polarity that pulls and tugs at you. Therefore, you have a need to make SENSE of these things that you call thoughts and emotions.

Once one gets out of the dimensions of corporeal bodies and duality and gets into the higher dimensions, the fifth and above, then one begins to see that thoughts and feelings are very REAL things. They are composed of energy. And ENERGY is a TANGIBLE commodity. When you begin to understand that you are dealing with a tangible commodity, you learn how to use it appropriately.

Thoughts and feelings become tools. They become helpers. They become ladders to greater awareness. We see them, these thoughts and things that you call feelings, just as you would see a tool in your hand.

Let's focus on this thing that you call feelings. We have feelings in our existence, too. However, we understand that we can work above and beyond techniques that involve duality; therefore, we do not have to manifest NEGATIVE feelings. Negative feelings are basically EMOTIONS, such as anger, guilt, fear, worry, hatred, and bitterness.

We deal with that feeling that you call LOVE. Love is a vibration, a positive vibration. We marry, so to speak, that feeling of love with what we are capable of doing with our thoughts. That love vibration allows us to enhance our thoughts because thoughts are also vibrations. Working in conjunction with one another, these two vibrations become incredibly wonderful tools.

Q. Have those entities in the eighth dimension released all of their old concepts, or are they still changing?

Are you asking if they are evolving like you? Absolutely! In the eighth dimension resides ALL THAT IS. Those who reach the eighth dimension are just those entities who have gone through the transitions necessary to bring them into that area where they can complete their training in ALL THAT IS. But there are still LEVELS of experiencing ALL THAT IS. Think of it in terms of your schooling. A person starts at first grade and graduates at the twelfth grade. There is a tremendous amount of opportunity for growth in between.

This is a free-will Universe for every entity. Every entity has the option of evolving and continuing to evolve. When one evolves through the dimensions in this Universe, one then moves into another universal area to experience even more growth.

So, there is ALWAYS shifting.

There is a greater sense of balance to this shifting in the higher dimensions — much more than you experience in your third dimensional consciousness. For you, change and growth are uncomfortable, painful, threatening, and challenging. For us, growth is exhilarating. It's freeing. It's peaceful. It has only positive aspects for us.

Q. We have learned that The Creator is androgynous, which is a perfect balance of male/female energy. What else can you tell us about The Creator?

The Creator is just as you are, as you ALL are. The Creator is the accumulative of ALL THAT IS. The Creator is imbalanced and balanced . . . because The Creator experiences through you, the co-creators. So, every molecule, every atom, every neutron, every proton of energy in The Creator resonates to every experience every co-creator has ever had.

The Creator is very different from that image you have created for yourselves. To feel comfortable and safe you created the "ultimate daddy," but you created the ultimate daddy for the third dimension. In our Universe, there are eight dimensions of consciousness. In other Universes there are greater dimensions of consciousness.

Contrary to the image you have created, The Creator

can dig down into that wellspring of neutrons, protons, and electrons and grasp every feeling that you've ever had to experience your same imbalanced feelings. And if The Creator chooses to dig down into that wellspring to experience balance, then so be it. So it is.

Why is it that you are afraid to believe The Creator can experience both balance and imbalance? Because you fear the loss of what you perceive to be the only constant, trustworthy element of your existence. When you understand that there is nothing YOU are not capable of, then there is nothing to fear.

It seems as if the very state of having imbalance with the balance is a type of a balance.

Yes, very well put. In understanding both sides of a concept or feeling, one understands it all. How could The Creator relate to those in the dimensions of duality if there were not the competence for duality within The Creator Him/Herself. The capability of experiencing imbalance is part of that competence.

Q. Will we ever reach a point when we don't have to fight "evil" in our efforts to stay balanced?

There is no such thing as evil in the Universe. There is no

evil in terms of what you think of it, either. You think of evil as satanic and of the devil. There is no such thing. Therefore, there is no battle against evil.

What you term evil is just a lack of understanding, a lack of awareness. There are only lower vibrations in which dwell entities and attitudes of heavier vibrations lacking in awareness and consciousness.

Neither is it necessary for those of higher consciousness to "save" those of lesser consciousness. In the absence of evil, there is no need for saviors. We are our own champions. We help others in our own level of consciousness by working on our own individual consciousness.

There is only OPPORTUNITY.

Q. What method of balancing is it most appropriate for us to be working with — some ethereal concept of balancing; some internal concept of balancing; body, mind, and spirit balancing; or balancing of our male/female aspects?

Primarily, humans feel a need to work with things that they can see, hear, taste, smell, or touch. It is through your senses that you tend to accomplish greater things. This is because you have those things called corporeal bodies.

Some people have a greater capability for thinking abstractly than others. You need to define for yourself where you stand in this ABILITY to think abstractly. If you are capable of thinking and working abstractly, then you are capable of working with more ethereal methods of accomplishing balance.

Think of those things of the spirit, which you presently think of as ABSTRACT, as VIBRATIONS of energy. Vibrations are something that you can literally control and manipulate. When you're capable of doing that, you're capable of negotiating your balance in a more effective way.

Q. The question that I have is about the use of magnets to keep the body in balance. If they are a valid tool, are they just useful for the physical, or does spiritual, emotional, and physical all combine?

Magnets are useful in connecting the life force with the body. They help the life force have greater input into the workings of the body. As such, they create better balance for you by drawing more power and energy from the life force into the human corporeal form.

Be careful not to "shoot from the hip" in using magnets. Use your insight. Use your ability to connect with transcendent information and transcendent entities to ensure that where you use them is appropriate for you.

Are magnetic mattresses good for the body?

It depends upon the entity. It depends upon the strength of energy being relayed by the life force into the body. Those entities who tend to be more balanced because their life force has greater input into their body, have less need for such a process. For others, it is a very good way of allowing the life force to fill the body and massage the organs and trigger points of the body during the sleep state.

How would a person know whether they are balanced to a point where they do or don't need magnets?

There are two ways to find out. You can try the device to see how it makes you FEEL. The other way is to talk to transcendent entities or your higher self and ask that very question.

Q. Now that it's become popular to be looking at our blood types for reasons of health and eating, is this something that also affects our balance?

From the beginning of that time when the human species was created, those teachers you had from other worlds who put you on your feet and then propelled you on your feet, spoke to you and taught you of these things. Then you started creating synthetic things. You started growing and eating things that were inappropriate for your bodies. Just as your dietary staples and supplements mutated (as they continue to do through chemicals in the modern day), so did your human bodies.

It is very important for balance that you eat appropriately. It is exciting for us to hear the knowledge that is opening up to you now about placing perspective on the blood flow and the type of blood that you have. For, eating in conjunction with the type of blood that you have is very appropriate.

Zachary, Sananda, Ezekiel

THE SYSTEM

My relationship and work with Zachary has been evolutionary both in form and content. When Zachary first started channeling information to me in 1993, he would stand beside me and "whisper" the information in my ear. Our work went on this way for over two years.

One day, as I was channeling for a client, I felt an unexpected surge of energy enter my body. My shoulders flew back and almost dislocated. I found myself squirming in my seat. At the same time, my client gasped loudly and demanded to know what "that flash of warm air" was that had just blown through the room. There was no easy way to explain the answer to that question.

At that time, Zachary's life force started merging with my body and my life force. Prior to this, I had asked Zachary to speak more directly through me. His merging with my life force and corporeal body was the first step in this process. My spiritual sophistication had just sprouted wings, literally.

Within minutes after our life forces would merge, Zachary and I would disconnect from my corporeal body. With Zachary serving as my navigator, we would then travel together to different dimensions and times.

Initially, Zachary's purpose was to teach me about the AKASHIC RECORDS. I had heard about the Akashic Records and knew, basically, that they were a cosmic record containing a history of ALL existence — past, present, and future. However,

I really didn't know in what form the records were retained, where they were retained, or how to access them. Zachary, knowing no limitations, took me right to the source.

Zachary is taking my hand. My uncle, Zachariah, is on the other side of me . . . of course with his beautiful wings. I feel like Peter Pan being whisked through the air. Smiling, Zachariah turns and looks at me. "Isn't reality grand?" he asks me. But it's really more of a statement than a question.

We have arrived at some sort of space station. I am told this is where the Akashic Records are kept. The curator of the records is walking through a doorway and handing us a crystal. The crystal is so large that I have to use both of my arms to hold it.

Zachary is now telling me to close my eyes. I can feel him lifting the crystal from my arms and placing it in my hand. Despite its size, I am able to close my hand over the crystal.

"See, Little One, anything is possible. Without limitations on your mind, in your brain, and in your heart, anything is possible."

I feel overwhelmed with the feeling and the possibilities that this belief brings . . . and the importance of sharing this understanding with others. I turn and look at Zachary with tears in my eyes.

He embraces me and says, "Welcome home to reality. Always keep this in mind as you're working amongst the things of the third dimension — keep your heart happy and light, and don't allow yourself to become overwhelmed. For, you can come here whenever you want. The doors are always open to you . . . to give you the courage and the conviction for your direction."

Zachary & Janis

I learned quickly from my interdimensional journeys with Zachary that our human bodies have the capacity to function without our life forces for a period of time without incurring physical harm or death. Moreover, all our human faculties are still operable. Therefore, I was able to transmit information from the Akashic Records THROUGH my body to my clients. What a trip!

Zachary and I took many extraordinary trips to the

Akashic Records. I discovered that by storing the information in crystal shafts the caretakers of the records could contain much more information more efficiently. The crystals were usually about two or three inches long and an inch in diameter — but there were exceptions.

At first, we would go inside the area that housed the records to get the crystal we needed for my client. There was a machine there. It was very large and round, made of some sort of material that looked like metal. It had a hole in the center of it that functioned somewhat like the chuck in a drill. I would place the crystal in the hole and tighten it like a drill bit in a chuck. Above the machine there was a huge screen, and the information from the crystal would flash on the screen like a video or movie. Over time and as my empathic abilities and confidence in myself grew, I learned to read the information in the crystal just by holding it in my hand.

My clients oftentimes wanted to know about their future. I discovered here, in the Akashic Records, that the future is only probable. That is because we live in a free-will Universe — one of the privileges and responsibilities of universal citizenship.

I liken future predictions to a cosmic computer that takes all the circumstances that exist AT THAT MOMENT and calculates the most probable outcome. Thereafter, our decisions and the decisions of others can alter this outcome.

This process of merging life forces with Zachary and going together to the Akashic Records proved to be quite effective. Zachary held firmly to the belief that I should always be part of the process — to empower me and assist in my own development. So, despite the fact that I gave him the option, Zachary would never agree to trance channeling.

Trance channeling is a process of channeling in which the host's life force leaves the body to give the entering life force total control. The entering life force becomes the dominant personality, usually speaking in a voice distinctly different from the host, and the host has little or no recall of what transpires.

The value Zachary places on EMPOWERMENT has taught me that true power comes from giving and allowing every citizen of the Universe their own power. In strengthening another, we strengthen ourselves — for we are all ONE. I have adopted Zachary's philosophy, and I now teach my clients how to channel their own information.

In the eyes of the Universe, it is critical that all of its citizenry be adept at two-way "cosmic communication" — channeling, empathing, and mediumship. This is particularly true now on the Earth, as its citizens will use this communication to help them in the TRANSITION into the next dimension of consciousness.

This process of conscious participation and empowerment has been preserved, even in the adding of the two other Transcendents (Sananda and Ezekiel) to our channeling team. However, with our duo turning into a quartet, a new system had to be developed. Have you ever tried to listen to three people at one time and take it all in? That can give you one major cosmic migraine.

What an exciting day it was for me, then, when the Transcendents introduced me to THE SYSTEM they had developed for us. It was July 19, 1997. The transition to this new system transpired during a group channeling I was doing that day.

As usual, Zachary merged with me. Our life forces shared one space with this body. Then we left my body and our life forces went through the cosmos together in merkabah bubbles *(see Cosmic Dictionary)*.

I felt as if I could reach out and touch everything I saw, even though we were going at warp speed. As we were going one direction, it was as though all the stars in the firmament were going in the other direction. They were like a blur of beautiful white light.

We arrived at the Akashic Records and were given the crystals with the information that was going to be channeled to the Starseed group this night.

Upon leaving the Akashic Records, I thought that I saw my uncle, Zachariah, because I saw very, very large wings. Then I realized it wasn't Zachariah at all. Zachary and I were sitting atop a tremendously big bird, like a condor, traveling through space. I remember looking and seeing these wings. They were so absolutely, incredibly huge — they must have been almost a mile wide.

The bird took us to the portal to the eighth dimension, where we were greeted by Ezekiel and Sananda. They told me that the reason we came to them in this way was to remind me that reality is an illusion — and we create our reality as we create our illusions. They explained to me that there are multiplicities of reality that we can create with our thoughts, and that one creation is as valid as any other.

At that point, we entered an open space filled with bright light. It felt safe and comfortable, yet efficient. It was not enclosed, and yet I felt that it was not entirely spacious . . . that at some point the spaciousness ended.

The Transcendents placed me under a crystal pyramid in the center of this "space." The pyramid was magically suspended in air, and it was the size of many Earth houses. Then each of the Transcendents stood at the three points under the pyramid and faced inward towards me.

Zachary stood at the point behind me, Ezekiel at the point to the right in front of me, and Sananda at the point to the left in front of me. Then they projected a tube of light to each other, forming a triangle of light around me. Finally, they projected tubes of light from each of themselves to me.

The tubes of light formed a communication network to transmit information and feelings between each of the Transcendents, which they then communicated through the tubes of light connected to me.

Through this communication network of light, all three of the Transcendents could communicate with me at the same time without breaking patterns of thought to shift from one Transcendent to the other. It also allowed them to speak with me individually or two-at-a-time. And it still enabled me to speak directly, when appropriate — to interpret information or symbols from them and to clarify information.

They demonstrated how this system also allows others to join us and share their thoughts and feelings. I was able to see them, hear them, feel their feelings, and develop a sense of their level of consciousness. For instance, in tonight's channeling, someone's mother wanted to speak to him from the other side of life through the portal of death. She was able to join us, step into the beam of light, and speak directly to him through me.

Similarly, this system allows the life forces of people still living upon the Earth to join us (their bodies can function for a time without their life forces, and it takes only seconds for their life forces to join us). Even beings from other dimensions and times can join us.

So, this system is what one could call an open mediumship and an open relationship, through which we can communicate back and forth. Each of us is empowered individually, and it allows me to be able to act as a channel in a multiplicity of ways.

With this system, there are no limitations.

Janis Abriel

Through this system, the Transcendents and I have shared many experiences. We have laughed together and cried together. But more importantly, we have shared information with others that they could use to enrich their lives. The Transcendents don't dabble in frivolous information, so I am always sure that whatever they share with me or my clients has significant meaning.

The Transcendents have taught me that we experience what we EXPECT, not what we WANT. Through my inter-dimensional journeys, I have witnessed demonstrations of how very capable we are of stepping out of such mediocrity and limited thinking . . . and into the extreme of beauty, love, truth, and joy-filled living.

CHANNELING

The Crystal City

"I want to take you someplace different this time," Zachary said to me. "This time, we're going to enter into the core of the Earth. Instead of going outward and up, we're going to go outward, down, and into the Earth — so that you can see the substance of the entity upon whose back you walk."

At first, I see what I would through my third dimensional eyes — what I EXPECT to see — thickness and ground.

But there is . . . oh, my gosh . . . there is so much more! There's an incredible, beautiful city! It's light, and white, and bright. It sparkles like crystal. It's many different colors. Like mother-of-pearl, it glistens and shines. It is pure and pristine.

Now Zachary and I are stepping down into the city. "Does it not surprise you? Does it not change your way of thinking to see things differently than as you expect them to be, Little One? Do you see that EXPECTATIONS hold you and your civilization down? There are no limitations. There is only beauty where we wish beauty to be, and there is darkness where we wish darkness to be. With the power of our thoughts, we can create anything."

"So it is here. We have created this beautiful city to exist within a higher vibration of frequency than those upon the Earth. There is intelligence here as there has never been elsewhere on the Earth. Here you will see the Transcendents walk amongst the humans . . . a hand-picked number of humans that we have brought here."

"This city houses some of the greatest minds that have ever existed upon the Earth. Here you will find the entities Einstein and Tesla working with some of the most beautiful, spiritual entities who have ever walked the Earth. Here is that oversoul of Sananda known as Gandhi. Here it is that Sananda walks within the Earth. There are many healers here. There are many councils held here. For here, in this place, these great people of knowledge and consciousness can accomplish much to help the Earth and the entities upon the Earth."

"This is a protected city. Your world government has agreed not to touch this city. They could, for they now know multi-dimensions. But it was agreed many years ago that there would be no interference, no injunctions, no control on their part. This agreement has been honored all this time."

Zachary and I are entering a courtyard. The beings who are here are light beings. They nod to us as they pass by. They've been awaiting our arrival. Yet, we are accepted with very little ado. It is a wonderful feeling to be recognized here.

I ask Zachary, "Why are we here in this particular place. Why do I see these entities?"

"You are here to know that there is much that exists beyond your every day EXPECTATIONS. This is a very important principle to teach those upon the Earth — there is violence in their lives . . . there is unhappiness in their lives . . . there is much confusion, quandary, and frustration in their lives . . . BECAUSE THEY EXPECT THERE TO BE."

"To accomplish what you have been sent here to the Earth to accomplish, teach these people to expect the best, the greatest, and the kindest. Let them know that NOW is the time to step out of mediocrity and into extremism — the extreme of beauty, love, and all the positive virtues."

"What you expect, you will manifest. So expect only those things of light, higher consciousness, truth, enjoyment, and pleasure. In this way, you will heal your Earth. In this way, you will heal one another."

"Make this Principle of Expectations a focus of your book. Make this a focus of your teaching."

Much to my dismay, Zachary informs me that it is time to leave. I ask him if we can come back. There's such a beautiful feeling here. It concerns me that I would not be able to experience this again. I want to come back when the time is right, for I know that such an extraordinary experience manifests only with a purpose.

Zachary & Janis

COSMIC CONNECTIONS
Part 1

I have learned from my own experiences and my close association with the Starseed that the blood that runs through all our Starseed veins is type C — Cosmic.

The way we think, feel, and function here reflects our cosmic genetics as much, or even more so, than our human genetics. The personality of the society and of our particular family on the planet we come from is the dominant factor in our personality here, regardless of the level of cosmic recall we have. Therefore, UNIVERSAL psychology must be employed in understanding the Starseed. Human psychology is, simply, not adequate to this understanding.

I was extremely fortunate to grow up with my seven brothers and sisters on the planet of Alcyone in the Pleiadian star system. We look very similar to you on Alcyone, although taller, and the substance of our form is ethereal. There we HONOR and enjoy all forms of existence, including animals and nature. Our planet is rich in foliage, water, and color. Our sky is teal in color, our life forces resonate well with royal blue, and even our animals have bright colors. Coincidentally, here on Earth my favorite color is teal; I look best dressed in royal blue; I plant vivid, multi-colored flowers wherever I live; and I'm devoted to my pets.

Everyone on Alcyone is empathic. Therefore, we are all

very honest and open with our feelings. This carries over for me here — I am very outgoing and wear my feelings "on my sleeves." I resent lies and secrets.

One of our dominant beliefs on Alcyone is that existence is to be enjoyed. Therefore, we create a positive environment of thought and activity and we have a very strong group consciousness. Because of this, we have no violence on our planet. I have, similarly, devoted myself here to peaceful and respectful forms of problem solving through my spiritual consulting and mediation practice.

"Back home," our families are the focus of our UNCONDITIONAL love. Those who choose to build their own family structure form a social commitment similar to marriage here. This relationship is afforded the highest respect, and it is considered a privilege to have the opportunity to form such a deep and enduring bond. Because of this, the domestic violence and infidelity so rampant here on Earth is totally foreign to my way of thinking.

I have some vivid memories of my own family and life on Pleiades. My strongest recall is of my father, Zachary. It was in my father's arms at the very young age of about five that I was told about my service to the Earth and taught my ability to succeed. We were on the planet Venus. There was warring and destruction going on all around us. I was terrified and clung to my father. His words rang clear in my ears that day, as they do at this very moment.

"Little One," he said to me, "just as you have survived this, you will have the strength to survive and succeed in your mission to the Earth. There will be difficult times, even times when you despair. But you will never give up . . . and you will fulfill your purpose." In fact, it is Zachary's confidence in me that has frequently given me the strength to go on.

My education began when I was very young with learning how to manipulate my environment with my thoughts. I moved on to spiritual development and the politics and psychology of the Universe. I remember fondly learning much of this from my mentor, "She Who Knows Most." We spent much time together in our "learning garden." We would walk within the beautiful floral surroundings to a building which looked quite similar to your Greek temples. We would sit there and talk. She would teach me with beautiful words of the mysteries and beauty of the Universe. It was such a pleasure to be with her and to learn from her.

As I matured on Alcyone, I marveled at the exceptional thought processes I saw develop in my older brothers' and sister's children. One of my most vivid memories is of a time when my brothers and sisters and I were entertaining five of my infant nieces and nephews with song and dance. We were all laughing heartily at our own antics. The children were far less amused, however. They dubbed us as "silly" and returned to chatting amongst themselves about more "important" things. For, even at this very young age, they could communicate fluently and had Einstein's principles down pat.

These little ones were EXTRA-ordinary. It had been determined by the Pleiadian Council of Elders that the life forces mother and father would bring into their family would be selected for their spiritual and intellectual capacities. Their children (my brothers, sisters, and I) would then be matched to our companions so we would be capable of rearing these extraordinary beings. With the approval and assistance of the Confederation of Planets, a crystal planet was created for them. The planet was designed to act as a transmitter to send the vibrations emanating from their life forces out into the Universe, thereby raising the vibrations and consciousness of all universal citizens. Some of my nieces and nephews are already fulfilling their PURPOSE on this crystal planet.

And what of their parents, my brothers and sisters? I have been in contact here on Earth with one of my elder Pleiadian brothers. I remember him with admiration and awe from our life together back home. I remember looking up to him and admiring his strength. He was tall and slender with broad shoulders — a presence to be reckoned with.

As happens sometimes in coming here to Earth, my brother forgot his strength and presence. He was born into a very critical family. He learned at an early age to close his hearing and feelings down. To avoid criticism and condemnation, he learned to lie. By the time we met in this Earth realm two years ago, he did not even resemble the presence I remembered.

After spending some time with my brother, I realized he was temporarily lost in the ways of the Earth. However, Zachary did not want to abandon this noble spirit. Despair sounded in his voice — the one and only time he has pleaded with me — when he asked me not to give up on my brother.

Zachary and I reached an agreement. To ensure that my level of vibrations was not brought down by this association, I cut the ethereal cord between my brother and myself — with the agreement that Zachary could reconnect it at any time he felt appropriate.

I have currently lost track of this brother, though I think of him often. I do take comfort in knowing, however, that his memory of himself will return as we go through the **TRANSITION** into the next dimension of consciousness. Then he will remember himself as I remember him and take his place with the other Starseed.

My youngest sister is also here on the Earth. She is a young adult now working on her own mission. She is also in contact with Zachary and our mother. It amazes me how much her Earth appearance resembles our mother.

My older sister and three other brothers are also here on Earth. But their story is very different. About thirty years ago, seven representatives from the Pleiades were sent to form an alliance with the Earth. They came here at the request of your world government, working in conjunction with the United States government. They were commissioned to prepare an agreement that would allow others from the Pleiades to educate your people in the ways of the Universe. When they arrived, instead of being greeted as emissaries, they were taken captive. I have vivid visual empathic recall of this incident from their memories. As I write this, the sobs are welling in my chest and tears are flowing down my face.

Because of their advanced abilities in forming and

manipulating energy, my brothers, sister, and their comrades have been kept at an underground military base. Here they are used for research to further the aims of your government and military organizations.

In 1996, I started having vivid visions of life forces in a glass enclosure. Their ethereal faces were pressed against the glass, horror and pain emanating from their eyes. At the time, I didn't understand the visions, but they haunted me everywhere I went.

A year later, an extraordinary experience prompted my recall of this entire story. My life force was taken spontaneously to a "concrete city" underground and adjacent to where my sister and brothers are being held. Here I was taught about the relationship between the Earth governments and those you call "extraterrestrials." Since then, my warehouse of knowledge on this subject has become vast. But nothing overwhelms my mind more than the indignity and injustice being suffered by these seven beautiful beings.

Mother, father, and I are allowed to visit my sister and brothers ethereally because it serves the research goals of these government and military organizations to keep their life forces functional. These visits are very difficult for father, sometimes reducing him to tears. Despite her gentle and sensitive nature, mother always appears determined and dignified at these meetings. Oftentimes she goes alone to spare father the trauma. Once father told me that it is mother's strength that has been the staff that has supported him through many experiences . . . that she just lets him look like the "strong one."

They've taken me there to them. I'm in the facility with them. They've been through much, but their spirits are strong.

They are saying to me, "Little sister, the thing that you can do to help us the most is to help the Earth and its people . . . for in raising their consciousness, we will be set free. Our story will be known, and there will be those who will set us free."

"Do your quest, and do it well . . . for therein is our hope of freedom."

Janis Abriel

My twin sister, Alcion, is the only one of my siblings who has not come to the Earth. It was agreed in my coming here, that she would always be able to accompany me in the ethereal realms — so that we would never be separated. It is her

And, so, I make this promise to you, my beloved brothers and sister and your valiant companions — that I will do my mission and I will do it well. In this book, I will tell your story . . . so that someday soon you will regain your freedom and return to us. I live every day of my existence here for the day I can take you home.

Janis

happy laugh and glowing smile that have been an integral part of my cosmic support system since coming here to the Earth. Alcion is outgoing and bubbly. A real chatter box, she always has something to laugh about. She has been my playmate and constant companion since our inception in Pleiades.

I referred briefly in the first chapter in this book to my cosmic companion, who was present at the time of my soul exchange. I talked about how difficult it was to leave him. I later described how we reconnected through my channeling. I identified him as Ezekiel and painted a picture of our relationship through the medium of words.

Both of our lives have been devoted to serving the Earth and its people. Yet, we have welcomed into our union (of over 200 Earth years) three life forces. Our oldest son is comparable in Earth age to six, our daughter to four, and our youngest son an infant.

When I go to the eighth dimension to channel, my children and I sometimes spend time, albeit brief, talking and soaking in one another's energy. On occasion, they even remain there with me during the channeling.

My three little children are here with me. They said to me, "Mommy, don't turn the tape on yet (I always record my channelings on an audio tape). We want you to be REALLY with us."

"Can you ever forgive me for leaving you to

come here?" I asked them.

"Oh yes, Mommy, there's no problem," they responded. "We're with you in the other dimensions all the time. You just don't remember that. And we want the tape to be off so that you can be with us and YOU can remember. We want you to remember, because WE remember when you're with us."

I reach down to them. My first response is to hug them, to put my arms around them and just squeeze them to me. And I do that. But then I realize that we can do more. So, we take our hands from our ethereal bodies and we touch our hands together . . . and the union of our life forces in this way and the joining of our energy in this way brings us all totally, completely together.

I have such a feeling of oneness with them. Although I can see that my three children are totally separate entities from me and that there are four of us . . . we are truly, in this process, of one mind and one heart.

Janis Abriel

In addition to the Pleiades, there are thousands upon thousands of other cosmic civilizations in our Universe. Each one is unique and lively in its own philosophies and activities. These different civilizations in the Universe call themselves clans. Regardless of what clan a Starseed comes from, he or she always comes to the Earth sponsored by an incredibly elaborate and efficient system known as **THE COMMAND**, which was described in detail in the chapter entitled "Finding the Starseed."

All the Starseed who come into your Earth must go through The Command to ensure that they are spiritually competent to be there.

Ezekiel

All Starseed are volunteers. They have undergone extensive training to accomplish specific missions while they are here. For instance, the Pleiadians usually bring with them the gift of love and higher consciousness; the Sirians are some of the greatest healers here; the Andromedans are here to assist the Earth in balancing the male and female energies; the Arcturians bring music and art with them; and, the Orions are masters at developing systems, plans, and technology. But ALL THAT IS is vast, so we have been joined by others from The Planet of Light, Hakubah, Solaria, Zanuba, The Crystal Planet, and many others . . . even some from other galaxies and universes.

It is because we come from the firmament to plant seeds of awareness and advancement that we are called "Starseed." Those here now either joined their human bodies at birth, or they were gifted bodies sometime in the course of their lives by their former occupants (these soul exchanges are always with the permission, and many times at the request of the former life force occupying the body).

To truly understand the Starseed, it is necessary to let go of the "Independence Day" and "Mars Attack" movie mentality. Most of us have forms, though ethereal, that are quite similar to human bodies. Many of our cultures are similar, or have been similar, to yours. We abhor violence, love nature, strive to serve, are natural healers, and cry with you at sad movies.

The Starseed are never alone here . . . though, sometimes they feel very lonely. The Command is aware of their every thought, feeling, and activity. It is not a "big brother is watching" scenario. Their guardianship is based upon unconditional love and concern for the Starseeds' well-being. They have one of the most incredible cheerleading sections in the Universe.

Because The Command has a very strict non-intervention policy with the Earth — to honor the universal Law of Free Will — Starseed are not above the challenges and heartaches faced by everyone on the planet. Their experiences also develop a base for mutual understanding between the Starseed and others on the Earth. I have shared with you some of my own challenges and heartaches, so you can see that what I say is true.

Whether they are consciously aware of their missions or not, those missions are the driving force behind everything the Starseed do. While a Starseed may punch a time clock, the everyday survival activities of providing a living are of secondary importance. Because they come from higher dimensions that don't revolve around the pursuit of money as they do here, ABUNDANCE has a much more spiritual meaning for the Starseed than for their Earthean friends and families.

CHANNELING

Abundance Is Relative

Q. Can you give us insight into this much-pursued state of existence we call "abundance" on our third dimensional Earth?

Abundance is relative. That relativity becomes much clearer as one's consciousness grows. As one is able to reach out and touch the face of God, one is far more capable of reaching out and touching the face on a dollar bill — because one knows where the value system is.

Money is a means to an end. Evaluate the end you're working for.

Q. Is there a balance to be maintained in manifesting abundance? That is, is there such a thing as "having too much?"

There is such a thing as WANTING too much of something.

There is balance to be maintained in every experience. As you move into the higher dimensions, balance becomes more prevalent. In your dimension, however, people are on different levels of wanting — some want very little, some want nothing, others want it all.

If you want something for inappropriate intent or inappropriate use, then there is such a thing as having too much of it. Look at your intent — is it to control others, feed your personal ego, or find acceptance from others because you can't find it within yourself? Then a penny would be too much.

Q. Why are many Starseed plagued with financial concerns?

Primarily, because they have less concern about finances than most people. Their lives in the higher dimensions didn't revolve around money as they do here. Money is literally "foreign currency" to the Starseed. It would be like going to another country and trying to learn the exchange system. For the Starseed, a monetary system is nonsense and useless. It has no significance, but it does have a tremendous amount of disadvantage if people's intent is inappropriate.

It is important to understand that the thinking of the Starseed supersedes the mundane. They have a whole different set of purposes and concerns. Because of that, they often have a resistance to dealing with money even when they have it.

This resistance is also due to the fact that money is a

manifestation, in many ways, of the lower vibrations of the third dimension. That doesn't mean there's anything intrinsically wrong with it. It just means that money has more potential for being abused and misused. Starseed sense this, and they have an aversion to misuse of anything.

Q. Is it a conflict of interest for the Starseed to have considerable wealth? Can they experience abundance and still accomplish their duties here on Earth?

The only conflict of interest would be if they don't know what to do with the money when they have it.

As with everybody, it's very important for the Starseed to be connected to INTEGRITY. There's a beauty in having money if the Starseed can use it for appropriate reasons.

Money can nurture one's soul in many ways. It can provide you opportunity — to be in a place where your soul can be nurtured; to be with people who can nurture your soul; to have the freedom to seek spiritual enlightenment without having to do the daily, energy-draining survival tasks.

The danger in having money is that the Starseed will put more energy into the getting, the taking care of, and the making more of it than into their missions. That would be the conflict of interest — if they don't know how to take care of it.

Zachary, Sananda, & Ezekiel

COSMIC CONNECTIONS
Part 2

Meeting the Starseed and learning more about them has been a fascinating process. Each one has found his or her way to me by hearing about my ability to identify those who come from elsewhere. They have sought me out because they felt "different" and displaced. More than anything, they sensed they had something specific to accomplish here and a time frame to accomplish it in. Their learning process has been mine. Through the "Starseed Readings" I have done, I have learned about a myriad of planets, cosmic civilizations, and the beings who populate them.

Initially, I secured the information about the Starseeds' planets of origin and their missions through my channeling. Now I sometimes take them through the dimensions and let them bring the information back to me.

These multi-dimensional journeys involve educating the travelers-to-be in the ways of the Universe, higher conscious-ness, altered states of consciousness, the Universal Mind, meditation techniques, and their own innate human and life force abilities. Then I serve as their navigator into the other dimensions. Because this is a fairly new — if not completely new — experience for these Starseed, most of their accounts are not as detailed as my own. Nevertheless, they have secured some information you might find quite interesting.

You will find that each account is unique. Collectively, this information is testimony to the diversity of our Universe. It is my hope that through this extraordinary information you will begin to appreciate the liveliness and the vitality of the Universe in which you live.

The human civilization is not an island unto itself. It is surrounded by other civilizations . . . existences as unique and interesting as your own. One of your sayings is that "variety is the spice of life." Now's your chance to get a very brief, but interesting, taste of it.

KAREN

Karen's interdimensional connection was with a planet called Shaalzar (sha-al-zar). There was a group of twenty-five beings there who communicated telepathically with her. She had an overwhelming sense that these beings functioned "egolessly." In here own words, this was her experience there.

"My name there is Shananda (sha-nan-da). My nickname is "Q." The planet I originate from is millions of light years away, much further than Andromeda. It has a silvery-blue hue. The surface is cold and barren, but we are not bothered by this. There are huge, beautiful structures of ice and crystals. There are several moons in a silver shiny-blue sky."

"We are called the 'celestial monks'. We are all dressed exactly the same in maroon robes with hoods."

"We all appear to be adult in age. We all have somewhat slanted eyes. The color of our eyes is deep brown-black. They appear almost as an infinite void — never beginning and never ending. They are as black liquid."

"My guide is a silver-white haired gentleman with a kind and gentle face. He has perfect features. All of my cosmic family have perfect facial features — humanoid-like and all dressed as monks."

"There is no mother or father, per se. We are all, actually, one infinite being. We are small silver-white balls of light that either manifest in this humanoid form for these discussions, or we become as ONE beautiful golden ball of light."

"We are advanced, pure spiritual beings, who spread compassion and non-judgment upon all planets, solar systems, and galaxies. We all have the name Shananda and each of us has a separate nickname."

"My mission is to spread non-judgment and unconditional love through the medium of music. It is a mission to unite all Earthlings in love and total acceptance — the ultimate goal being a return to SOURCE, a re-connection with The Eternal Creator."

LORETTA

Loretta's interdimensional visit was to the planet Tyron (tie-ron). She felt no familial ties there, but she believed it to be the planet where she was prepared for coming here to the

Earth. In her own words, here is a description of what she experienced there.

"My planet is purple and green. It is a planet of scholars. The people are very tall with very large foreheads. They are all dressed the same in kind of an oriental style. There are no outward shows of affection, no hugging or touching. This is all done with the mind."

"This is where I was taken and trained. I was to experience many things so I could relate to the people on Earth — to heal them and raise their consciousness. I am to help all I can during the TRANSITION."

SELENE

Selene is from what she called The Crystal Planet because it was "full of crystals." Here is what she experienced on her interdimensional visit to her planet of origin.

"I met Abraham, my guide, at a pool. He came walking over to me. I stood up and looked at him. He was dressed in a beautiful red velvet robe. He had beautiful curly hair and a beard. His eyes were dark and full of love and humility. The more I asked questions, the more humility I saw in his eyes. Our creation interconnected. We became one."

"We entered the portal and the light shield around us propelled us into the cosmos. We appeared on a planet full of crystals. All around the planet, there was a beautiful deep blue. Our planet glistened against the dark blue."

"Soon, there were entities that began walking toward

us. They all wore gowns. Two emerged more strongly than the others. It looked like my mother and father. She was called Therra and he was called Far. "

"I knelt down on one leg before my parents. My mother placed her left hand on the left side of my head. My father placed his left hand on the right side of my head. Then they each placed their right hand under my chin and bade me to arise, and we faced each other. My face was very important. They called me Inuah (i-new-a)."

"When Abraham and I left them, we stepped into a shaft or tube of light. We moved away from them very fast . . . then into a spiral back to the pool site. I placed the shaft of light in the crypt behind my bench at the pool."

IRA

Ira's visit was to the planet Zyon (zi-on). There he found a tall stick-like figure inside a bright yellow orb. After a while, there were many such beings. They moved forward and materialized slowly. All of their features were similar, though different genders were apparent. They did not speak to Ira until toward the end of their meeting when one of them counseled him on his personal work.

JILLIAN

Jillian was unsure of the name of the planet she visited. She said it sounded like Cyron, Cylon, or Surrus. The planet had a large flamingo-colored sun. Stars of light were sparkling and fog-like clouds of white gold could be seen in the sky.

The planet emanated the colors blue, white, and white-gold from its surface. Jillian could see a garden with a fountain of water running over smooth, deep blue stones and rough black rock. There was also a structure made of amethyst crystal that had tall spires.

The beings Jillian saw first appeared as bubbles of light. When communicating with her, they would take form as long, thin bodies of light that looked something like marble statues. Jillian told us, "They took my head in their hands to communicate. Their eyes were golden like a tiger's or leopard's. I got the idea from them that I was to be light and love and spread such."

I have seen hundreds of other cosmic connections in the channelings I have done myself for other clients. To conclude this chapter, I will include a few of these "Starseed Readings" I have done for clients.

TRACY

We discovered, through the Transcendents that Tracy is one of a very few beings on the Earth from the planet Hakubah (ha-coo-ba). There she is called Mesmera (mez-meer-a).

Tracy's people had their roots in the "Wise One." The Wise One came to Hakubah from another planet for a specific purpose — to begin a civilization devoted to growth in consciousness through the practice of SERENITY.

The Wise One brought with him to Hakubah a female being from another planet. She was of high social status in a civilization that had not-so-much serenity as her male companion. The Hakubans smilingly refer to the mother of their race as the "Wisest One."

Both of these beings, though from very different clans and backgrounds, were devoted to the concept of developing this civilization with its roots well established in ACTIVE SERENITY. As a result of this foundation, the Hukubans are now in the seventh dimension of consciousness.

Because of their level of consciousness, the Hakubans are beings of very high and light vibrations. As a result, they appear "wispy," almost pencil thin. They float rather than walk and never appear to come in contact with the surface of their planet.

Their heads are elongated, wider at the top. Their faces are placid when they are moving or in the process of performing activities. But, a tremendous change takes place when they communicate telepathically — their faces become lively with expression, their eyes glow and twinkle, and big smiles mirror their internal joy and pleasure in "community."

The Hakubans have an extraordinarily strong group consciousness which they are very comfortable with. Therefore, there are no castes. Equality reigns, and violence has no reason for rearing its head.

These are a peaceful, loving, friendly, and harmonious people, intimately familiar with the nature of their life forces. They live quite simply with a few, very beautiful possessions. When we visited them, they all appeared to be wearing richly woven robes of metallic olive green and black with long, bell-shaped sleeves. They do have animals, which like them, are small and fragile, but strong in spirit.

To ensure the continuity of their devotion to the practice of serenity, new life forces are welcomed into this clan as youthful members rather than as adult entities. This allows the Hakubans to teach this principle from the inception of the new member's life force into the clan. This is more effective than having to integrate this practice into an already established adult personality with pre-conceived ideas and devotion to other ideals. The children are raised in a space of serenity and respect in the ways of the Wise One.

Hakubah is a planet, but it is so bright that it is often mistaken for a star. It almost looks like glass. It glows and its surface is smooth. Projecting from the surface is something that looks like glass mountains. There is very little greenery, and that was brought from another planet.

The Hakubans are a comparatively small colony of beings, so most of the planet is uninhabited. They say their cities are very "harbored." That means they are enclosed, like cities in a bubble of glass.

They like their lives organized — arranged nicely and tidily. Their environment is set up to allow them an atmosphere of peace, gentility, and softness. Their existence is quiet, sublime, respectful, and honorable. They create their environment through their thoughts.

One of Tracy's guides is an entity from the planet Hakubah. He is an androgenous (balanced male-female energy) being by the name of Masua (ma-soo-a). In his own words, this is his reason for serving as her guide.

> "I am here to help you find the calm in the eye of the hurricane . . . to guide you through difficult times. Because we are from the same place, our relationship will re-connect you to your sense of serenity, peace, and higher consciousness."

> "Go. Be by yourself. Call my name and have no expectations. You may hear me at that time. You may hear me in the sound of the wind. You may hear my voice clearly in your head. You may hear me in the babble of the stream, or when you turn the water on in the sink. You may hear me when you look into the eyes of others. But my voice will always be there whispering encouragement and greater ways to you . . . and breathing peace into your heart and soul."

> "Stay grounded and centered. Try to keep your vibrations at a constant speed — not the ups and downs of hills and valleys, but at a constant speed. In so doing, you will re-connect with the vibrations of our people and the serenity that affords you."

MARIE

Marie most recently spent several hundred years on a planet called Baorjane (ba-or-ja-nay) in the Pleiadian star system. It is considered to be a "place of much brilliance and light." Baorjane is in the seventh dimension of consciousness.

Marie is from a unique sect of beings known as the "Letter Writers." The Letter Writers are highly literate and articulate. They serve as the historians of the Pleiadian system, recording and maintaining the records of all history pertaining to the past, present, and future of that system. Right now, their work includes documenting the involvement of the Pleiadians in the Earth existence.

The Letter Writers are a peaceful and serene people, but they have a playful side. They number just in the hundreds. They were individually chosen by the Pleiadian Council of Elders to do this work, because each Letter Writer is very enlightened, insightful, and extraordinarily empathic. They all have a remarkable ability to FEEL the facts of their research, as well as understand them with praiseworthy accuracy.

The Letter Writers are distinctive among the Pleiadians. In addition to being very, very tall and slender, they have foreheads that slant backwards. They chose to be unique in this way because "it denotes autocracy." According to them, "It's important to understand that we're all unique, even within a group consciousness. We wanted to always remember to honor differences and to accept them. It also identifies us as the Letter Writers, as the historians." This distinguishing mark is similar to press badges. It identifies them and gives them autonomy to do their work wherever they go among the planets.

Marie came to Earth as a representative of the Letter Writers during the Earth's TRANSITION into the fourth dimension of consciousness. Until now, she has been preparing for this mission by experiencing many different things — activities, philosophies, people, and avenues of working with people — to develop a perspective of what the Earthean existence is like. During her mission here, the other Letter Writers serve her as protectors, guides, and "encouragers."

Because of her own strong spiritual connection, Marie sensed that she had a strong connection with the Orion star system, as well. Her insight led us to the knowledge that while her most recent cosmic connection was with the Pleiadian system, her cosmic family and her most vivid cosmic roots were on the planet Zanebula (za-neb-u-la) in the Orion system.

Her people, meticulous and detailed, keep historical records for the Orion system. She was actually recruited by the Pleiadian system because of her successful work background on Zanebula.

The Zanebulans can manifest anything they choose because they exist in a very high dimension of consciousness. Yet, they choose to manifest simplicity in their lives. They are a peaceful, loving, gentle, and gracious people. In addition to exhibiting these qualities, Marie was also a little on the "feisty" side, contributing to her ability to secure necessary information for the historical records.

Like the Letter Writers on Baorjane in the Pleiades, the Zanebulans are a unique sect (although, not all the Zanebulans are historians). The Zanebulan historians also manifest a unique form — the left side of their tall and humanoid form is light orange and the right side of their form is a dark orange — to remind them to accept and honor differences. In fact, this Principle of Acceptance is a very important philosophy among these people, as well as with the Letter Writers.

On Zanebula, Marie is known as Mauriana (mar-e-a-na). She comes from a very large family with many siblings. Her brothers and sisters are performing a variety of functions in many different parts of the Universe. Her parents chose to manifest her siblings as infants (rather than bring them into this experience as adult life forces), so they could be raised in the ways of Zanebula.

Her father is a very big person, a strong and powerful male energy, leader, and decision maker. Her mother, called Harisima (ha-ris-e-ma), is a nurturer and teacher, and she is known as being "full of love." The name Harisima, like many in the Universe, can't be pronounced with the human vocal chords. The Transcendents call this a "sounds-like" name.

HADUYAH

A nebula in the Orion System is home to Haduyah . . . more specifically, a planet in the system known as Ofrazentaura (off-ra-zen-tar-a).

Her people are described as the "fleet" or the "quick"

because they move with incredible speed. In fact, they are light beings who move so quickly interdimensionally that "it takes your breath away." For that reason, they have been assigned as the "Gate Watchers" of the interdimensional portals — to ensure the integrity of the energy in each of the eight dimensions. This is a unique clan and small in numbers.

Haduyah's mission here on Earth is directly related to the capabilities of her cosmic relations. She is here to preserve the integrity of the energy on the Earth after its TRANSITION into the fourth dimension. She will be doing a specific type of energy work involving the healing of individuals and the Earth. The purpose of this is to bring the Earth and its inhabitants up to their best fourth dimensional standard.

Haduyah was counseled to be creative and think of new methods of working with the energy of people and the Earth. The Transcendents' own words to her were, "The waters will need to be smoothed. Remember these words. You will understand them."

After this Starseed reading, Haduyah told me of a vision she had about a year before. She described it as being "in her spiritual mind." She was living in Georgia at the time. Her apartment looked out over the complex's parking lot. Sometime between 2:00 and 3:30 in the morning, she saw an oval, metallic-silver UFO land in the parking lot. A man with dark, golden skin wearing a dark jump suit stepped out of the craft.

The man entered her apartment. He told her, "Do not be afraid. We are just making contact with you." He had something that looked like a telephone in his hand. He was communicating with someone through the device as he was talking to her. She heard him tell the person on the other end of the communicator, "The best way for us to come is by water." He then left.

The use of the word "water" in both of these instances seemed more than a coincidence to Haduyah and I, but we were confused about what the entity meant by "coming by water." So, a couple of weeks later, I channeled some more information to clarify his meaning.

We were told that water was an analogy for "vibrations." What he said was, "We will have to come in at a certain energy vibration" and "The vibrations will need to be smoothed after the TRANSITION into the fourth dimension."

In fact, during his face-to-face encounter with Haduyah, the entity was tuning into her energy. His intent was to determine what vibrations it would be necessary for him and his other-dimensional comrades to enter into when coming to assist in the Earth's TRANSITION into the fourth dimension. As he explained, "If she could see me [my vibrations], then we could bring the same experience to others."

Who was this entity and did he have any other reason for manifesting to Haduyah? That question was clarified for us in the channeling, too. We were told he was a representative from The Command, sent out in a "scout ship" to look for potential Earthean assistants to help them during the TRANSITION. During the time he spent with her, he was tapping into her mind to determine how much she was able to absorb of what he told her, her level of consciousness, and her ability to work with and experience his vibrations. We were told she passed the exam.

During their initial encounter a year ago, this representative from The Command also presented Haduyah with three babies wrapped very tightly in blankets. Haduyah asked me to clarify the significance of this for her during one of our channelings. We were told that the babies represented the birth of our Earthean movement into the fourth dimension of consciousness. Each baby represented an opportunity or choice Haduyah could make in the TRANSITION. She was reassured that she would know what those choices were at the time of her "Quickening" *(see Cosmic Dictionary)* during the TRANSITION. She was counseled not to be concerned about the matter in the meantime.

CHANNELING

Remembering Your Cosmic Family

"I, The Creator, am also here to see the things that transpire . . . to inspire you to nobleness and to the fulfillment of prophecy that stands in our Universe . . . that you will bring this Earth to a place of joy, to a place of holiness, to a place of giving, respect, and honor."

The Creator

Q. The Starseed come from many different planets and star systems in our Universe. How important are these "home cultures" to each of the Starseed?

These "home cultures" have fed the knowingness of the Starseed who are upon the Earth and literally determined their missions.

Those Starseed from Pleiades come to instill love and raise the vibrations through raising the consciousness. Those from Sirius come to help the Earth entities heal their hearts, their souls, their minds, and their bodies so they can become whole and united. These are only two examples. But the abilities of EVERY Starseed are derived from their level of vibration — and that level of vibration resonates with the culture of their planet.

Therefore, The Starseed and their cosmic homes are inextricably connected. They cannot be disconnected. The Starseed are, in fact, more representative of their cosmic cultures than any associations on Earth. That is why they feel so at odds, at times, with their existence on Earth.

Q. Is it helpful for the Starseed to know about their cosmic families?

For some it is very important. In many cases, the cosmic families are very involved with their Starseed members. They have made commitments to serve as guides and as angels. They communicate in what you call "that still small voice" that you respond to intuitively.

These cosmic families, at the very least, are connected through vibrations to their members upon the Earth. The MEMORIES, even dormant, of the love within these families — of the challenges they have gone through together, of the growth they've experienced and of the culture and philosophies they have shared — and how that all blends together to bring the

Starseed to this point of standing upon the Earth cannot be underestimated.

In some cases, memory of their cosmic families may make the Starseed yearn more for their cosmic homes. If they can overcome this yearning by understanding that they volunteered for where and who they are at this time, this remembrance is appropriate. Then they will have no need to cling to their cosmic families. Then their desire for cosmic connection will be for the appropriate reason — because the vibrations from that connection can enlighten and guide them.

Q. Are these cosmic families eternal, or do the Starseed progress from one cosmic family to another?

Cosmic families are eternal in that the connections through the VIBRATIONS are eternal.

Entities may choose to incarnate in a variety of different places to learn the vibrations and the lessons available to them through those existences. Just as you travel from one country to another to experience each country's unique culture and dynamic force, so can the Starseed experience the unique cultures and opportunities of the various planets and star systems.

Entities, who choose to be eclectic learners, have the opportunity to join other family units in various parts of the Universe as part of their learning process. So, while there are some entities who continue always upon their same planet of origin, others have experienced multiple "incarnations" and have multiple planets of origin.

These incarnations are not the same as you experience. You think of incarnations in terms of the physical body. Incarnations in the fifth through eighth dimensions of consciousness are accomplished with an ethereal body. Ethereal entities may begin their growth as, what you call, children, or they may join a cosmic family as an adult.

Q. If a Starseed has had multiple planets of origin, would there still be one that he or she would call home or resonate with more than the others?

Starseed, who have had eclectic families, bring ALL of what they have learned through those relationships and experiences with them to the Earth. These Starseed feel multiple connections to the Universe. They may, however, resonate more to one planet of origin than another based upon the specific mission they have chosen to fulfill and where they developed the skills for performing that mission.

Q. Is there anything else you would like to share with the Starseed about their cosmic families or relationships?

We understand the incomparable separateness and

aloneness that our beautiful Starseed can experience in this third dimensional vibration. For that reason, understanding your belovedness to your cosmic family can actually raise your vibrations and help you understand more clearly who you are. This cosmic "boost" can give you the understanding, the strength, the determination, and the motivation to fulfill your missions . . . and to assist the Earth through this TRANSITION into the fourth dimension of consciousness.

Connect with your cosmic families with PURE INTENT. That intent is to experience successful missions.

Zachary, Sananda, & Ezekiel

THE FOURTH DIMENSION

The information I've gathered about the Starseed, including myself, whether through Starseed readings, other channelings, empathing, medium communications, or other interdimensional travels, have brought me to the doorway of another reality. The sign on that door reads, "ENTRANCE TO THE FOURTH DIMENSION."

Every cosmic connection whispers in our Starseed ears, "You're not from Earth, but you have a purpose in being there — a mission. You volunteered for that mission. You trained for that mission. You're still training through your Earth experiences and ethereal life force communications with us. Your training is almost completed. In the following months, you will be called upon to use your individual skills and your collective consciousness to assist the Earth and its inhabitants in transitioning into the fourth dimension of consciousness."

"This will not be an easy mission to accomplish. You will experience personal sorrow and grief. You will witness much destruction, death, and chaos. Even now, the wheels are in motion. Some of you are already serving in preparation. We ask you to remember THE BIG PICTURE as you wipe the tears from your soiled cheeks. The Creator has told you, 'There is always more.' And, so there is. Beyond the temporary destruction lies destiny."

"Your Earthean brothers and sisters will be cradled in the loving arms of the fourth dimension. They, too, will dry their tears when they see their Earth in its natural state and their bodies healed by higher vibrations. They will revel in the power their thoughts evoke. When you see them dance in the streets of destruction and destiny, you will have succeeded."

When I began channeling information about this TRANSITION into the fourth dimension in May of 1997, I would ask the Transcendents to give me a specific time when this TRANSITION would occur. Initially, they told me we were to focus on raising our consciousness and not be concerned with a specific time.

In February of 1998, the Transcendents told me about five events that would take place leading up to the TRANSITION. In July of 1998, they cautioned me, "It's much closer than you think." Then they started showing me specific events a few days or weeks before they occurred — fires in Florida, the tsunami that killed 3,000 people in New Guinea, and the bombing of the American embassies in Kenya.

Something different occurred, however, when I was given the vision of the embassy bombings. In addition to a picture of the scenes — the buildings, the debris, the cloud of dust — I experienced intense emotions of grief. I felt the death, the confusion, and the disbelief. I began sobbing. I continued crying for days. Even now, I experience that grief when I re-enter this vision. It was as real for me as if I had been there.

I believe, from these visions and the words of imminency the Transcendents have shared with me, that THE TIME OF THE TRANSITION IS NOW. I believe the Transcendents counseled us well a year-and-a-half ago to work on our consciousness. To have given us a time frame then would have only caused alarm and fear. Now that the TRANSITION is in progress and the most significant phenomena are imminent, it is time to brace ourselves for the impact.

It is not my purpose to present you with any "doom and gloom." You can get those doomsday reports from television, radio, voices from the past, and other written words that say you are on the brink of experiencing the end of the world.

It is my purpose to present you with reality. This TRANSITION is part of THE PLAN you, I, and The Creator put together. Do you remember what The Creator said to you earlier in this book? You are the Creator's FOOTSTEPS. Your ethereal feet have taken you into the first, second, and third dimensions of consciousness to "experience and create the grandest potential." Those experiences have provided you the opportunity to test your ethereal stamina and flex your ethereal muscles.

Now you are ready to graduate from the third dimension where Gaia, the Earth, has been your classroom; your EXPERIENCES have been your course of study; your final exam is on The Principle of Acceptance; and, the result of your final exam is determined by the quality of your COLLECTIVE CONSCIOUSNESS. That collective consciousness determines WHAT you experience in your TRANSITION into the fourth dimension. Your INDIVIDUAL consciousness determines HOW you experience your TRANSITION into the fourth dimension.

Right now, as a collective consciousness, your invention has exceeded your compassion. You are using your technology to hurt instead of help one another. Your material desires outweigh your spiritual insight.

In the home of ALL,
they were overcome with the splendor
of GAIA's offer.

"To honor you, GAIA,
we will give this place your name," ALL exclaimed.

"I ask only that you honor the differences
between you,
as you walk upon my back,"
GAIA responded.

"But, GAIA, we have never done this before.
What if we forget who we are,
and lose sight of our promise to you?"

"Then I will remind you.
If should ever the heavens be caused to weep
because of your forgetting,
I will send Antithesis upon the back of
Loyal Whale to dry her tears.

Seeing this, you will be reminded to
SEARCH FOR YOURSELF
IN THE RUINS OF YOUR DIFFERENCES."

Zachary

Remember, this TRANSITION is part of YOUR PLAN. As The Creator said earlier, "It is intended and part of the plan that YOU CREATED that this would take you into a greater understanding of existence." The Transcendents also want to remind you "that those of you that stand upon the Earth at this time chose to stand upon the Earth at this time and be a part of this [TRANSITION]."

You are linked to one another here upon the Earth through the human DNA you inherited from Adam and Eve. You are linked to ALL of existence through the cosmic DNA you inherited from The Creator, the progenitor of your life force. Therefore, all of existence has a stake in your making this TRANSITION in the best possible way. Play that trump card now. Use the information you get from transcendent spiritual forces to guide your way into and through the fourth dimension. Zachary, Sananda, and Ezekiel give you this confidence:

**Spirit speaks,
and it speaks *wisely*.**

**Spirit speaks,
and it speaks *nobly*.**

**Spirit speaks,
and it speaks *with awareness*.**

Spirit speaks
with questions
. . . and then answers them.

"Listen to your spirit.
Focus less on the things of your body now,
and more on the things of your spirit
. . . and you will be prepared."

You have probably heard a number of predictions about this long-awaited event. The Transcendents tell us that The Plan is in motion and it is flawless. Here is their insight into our **TRANSITION** into the fourth dimension, and what we can expect when we arrive.

. . . And so it is with this TRANSITION . . . that it will be something that appears at first dark and ominous. In fact, you will not lose sight of yourselves in it. Once you overcome the fear and the feeling of strangeness that surrounds you from what is happening, you will want to soak it in . . . you will want to breathe it in . . . you will want to pull it into your body as rays from the sun.

You will see around you that things are going to be happening . . . that things are going to be changing. You know that what is transpiring here is that the things of the past, the things of your past, the things of the old world, the things of the old ways, are literally falling down around you. But there is no fear in this. There is no feeling of loss or grief in losing these things.

And you watch . . . you watch in awe and wonder. At first you are unsure of what the purpose of it is. But then peace — the voice of peace — speaks in your heart and in your head. It tells you that you are not losing things around you that are of import . . . these are just THINGS that are going to fall to the wayside . . . because they have no value anymore.

Those people who deny their curiosity and choose to react out of their fear may encounter that process you call death. Those entities who have a lesser understanding of themselves, of their own creatorship, are the beings who will be more fearful.

Understand that death is only that of the human body; it is not that of the life force. So, you will see beings of light standing around you. Though their bodies may lie at their feet, they too will experience this TRANSITION fully. In their light bodies, they will be able to assist you in your building for a period of time — until it is either their time to reincarnate or to go on through the portal and await the process of reincarnation into the new body form of this Earth existence.

Then you will find yourself AS THOUGH waking up from a

dream. You will see that the Earth has returned very much to her primordial state. There are beautiful things around you — trees, grass, bushes, plants, and flowers — unlike anything you've ever seen. Even your desert regions will be filled with abundance of life.

The animals will sound their joy through their voices. You will hear their chatterings. You will hear their chirpings. For the birds will be flying in an air free of pollutants. They can even ride on the vibrations of your atmosphere because your air is now pure.

Not only have the things of your atmosphere and your Earth changed, but also the vibrations around you. They're lighter. They're brighter. You hear the sound of joy in these vibrations. And you don't feel fear.

You're excited. As you look around, you see that there are many others who have awakened to see this . . . as though they have awakened from a sleep. In fact, what they have done is walked through a portal. The portal from one dimension to another. It is a feeling that they have come from a dream state, from a sleep state. In fact, they've walked from one vibrational state into another.

In these vibrational states, there are feelings of awe and wonder. People are dancing and laughing. They have no sense of loss. They have no sense of fear.

They embrace one another. There are no longer the artificial barriers that humans had put up between themselves.

They embrace each other, and they laugh, and they talk. They talk about what this means. They talk about what the opportunities are that exist here and how they shall build upon this. They know that they must never again cover the Earth and her pores with cement . . . nor put sounds in her vibrations that are negative . . . nor depreciate their new home with thoughts that are negative.

They know this is a time of evolution, a time of beginning, a time of building again — knowing all the things of the past — but only wanting to bring into the present the things that are those of peace, beauty, joy, and oneness.

It is truly a NEW BEGINNING with all of the OLD UNDERSTANDINGS . . . that allow you to make more appropriate choices . . . to honor the Earth . . . and to understand the Earth as it truly is — an enlightened being who formed himself into this creation so that you may walk upon his back to have your experiences . . . to experience your JOY. Now you understand that fully and you want to treat Gaia, the Earth, with respect and honor. You learn, now, how to talk to Gaia and communicate with him.

You learn to communicate with one another now in a way that does not know the barriers of fear, violence, retaliation, and rejection. You need not even open your mouths to communicate if you don't want to. You can communicate through the vibrations of your thoughts with one another.

Your first thought is that you must control your thoughts because you don't want other people to know what you're thinking. Then you realize that these are beautiful vibrations around you. Your thoughts are of the higher things. Your thoughts are of building great and beautiful things . . . and there is nothing to hide now . . . nor has there ever been. Now you realize that.

You see in front of you OPPORTUNITY to build a brave new world — opportunity to reach out and touch one another without the use of your telephone lines. Now you can reach out and touch one another with pure and undefiled hands, with pure and undefiled thoughts.

Now you see in your daylight sky that there are stars and moons. You can see these — the stars and moons that, heretofore, you have only been able to see in the dark. You can see them with your eyes fully opened, for the vibrations in your mind have changed to encompass existence more fully . . . as it is in the Universe. You no longer need to experience day and night to experience it ALL.

Here in this world, you do not have the need to experience opposites as you did in your other world. Here you can experience more. Here is your stepping stone. Why is it you can experience it this way? It is because your body has changed. The vibrations have raised so that your human brain is no longer a barrier to your kinship with the Universe.

Your body vibrates at a higher rate. Therefore, you have the ability to regenerate it. You do not have the mass body that you had before. It is no longer opaque. It is more translucent and transparent, as are your thoughts. Because of this, your connection with the Universe is greater. For this reason, you can see the stars and the moons in your daylight skies.

Your intentions here are noble. Your intentions are as builders. You all want to build a temple in which to live . . . this temple being one of higher consciousness and understanding.

Now you ask, "Are we alone or are there others here — others not quite like us?"

You see around you that, yes, there are others . . . others that you didn't see before. You see the Starseed for who they are — entities who came here to encourage you and to help you through this period of TRANSITION and building.

You see that there are others from out in the Universe . . . others that you've not heretofore experienced.

They come in peace, unlike what you would have expected in your other existence. You're excited. You want to talk to them. You want to learn from them. You want to incorporate them into your civilization. So you shall . . . if you choose to embrace this beautiful existence that is now your opportunity.

You are no longer limited to the understanding or the belief that you are the only race in the Universe. You realize that there are many other races in the Universe (or, as we call them, "clans"). These clans will come to you as you need them, as it is appropriate for you to learn and grow. They will come to you on an individual basis, in group and social settings, and at times and places that are appropriate.

You need not be afraid. For, you now know that these are your brothers and sisters from the sky . . . and that you are part of their existence, as they are part of yours. They will teach you how to reach further out into that sky . . . for, now you have a great desire to touch those stars, to walk upon them, to experience them in a completely different way . . . to embrace them in your hearts and souls like you've never understood before.

You will learn many new things — many new things about how to travel to these places and times where you can experience these things. Here your consciousness will open to the understanding of time and other dimensions.

Again, you are individuals and some of you will grow and build at faster rates than others. You will allow this for one another. For, as you walked through that vibrational force into this dimension, this new home of yours, you truly experienced that PRINCIPLE OF ACCEPTANCE that was brought to you in your last existence through that entity you call Jesus the Christ, known in the Universe as Sananda. Now you can embrace ACCEPTANCE completely in your heart, and mind, and soul.

Will you experience that entity who brought you this gift? Yes, you will. For, Sananda will be at your doorstep, too. You will experience him now fully — not only in form but in being. During a space of time (of days), Sananda will teach you. He will be experienced in many places at the same time — through the force of his oversouls, his being, and his energy — he will reach everyone with his teachings.

Sananda will be joined by others, including his father (the one that you have oftentimes referred to as the Father in the trinity . . . the Son being Sananda . . . and the Holy Spirit being the vibrations upon whose back their words will go out to touch everybody). There will be many others — multitudes of others — to help you understand, to teach you individually and in groups . . . to prepare you.

Then they will leave. The challenge will be yours to take what you've learned and to go forward and build that brave new world. In the building of that, you will build your way into the next dimension.

And so it is . . . THE BEGINNING.

Zachary, Sananda, & Ezekiel

NOW IT IS TIME FOR YOU TO EXCHANGE REALITIES:

... to experience Earth changes and soul changes

... to discover new opportunities

... to meet your brothers and sisters in the sky

... to learn that there is always more

... to build your consciousness

with the help of the spiritual

insights the Transcendents

have shared

in this book.

I wish you a wonderful journey

to and through your new reality

... YOU, the blessed FOOTSTEPS of The Creator.

Janis Abriel

Nigh Is The Day

THE GODS WILL
ARRIVE ON OUR
DOORSTEPS

So we who have for lifetimes prepared
   ... Will open our hearts and minds to What Really Is
   ... And set aside our Fear ... and Ignorance ... and
      Superstition.
And when we pass thru the Portal of Darkness & Light
   ... That brings our bodies to etherea
   ... Our watches to a stop
   ... Our minds to YES
   ... And our planet to its destiny

WE WILL ARRIVE AT THE DOORSTEPS OF THE GODS!

Janis Abriel

THE COSMIC DICTIONARY

ABDUCTEE — A person who has experienced "being taken" aboard an extraterrestrial space craft for the purpose of genetic research, behavioral observation, and/or "cosmic" education. The abductee phenomenon began centuries ago as the result of agreements between a number of governmental and military agencies on Earth and an extraterrestrial clan known as the "Greys." The Greys made the initial contact with the Earth because they needed to combine our human genetics with their own to avoid extinction. These government agencies "loaned" a number of their human citizenry for this purpose in exchange for the Grey's technology.

The abductee phenomenon has a dual nature and result, as all other Earthean experiences do. Abductees may experience sporadic memories that incude confusion and trauma or even pleasant and insightful contact with these extraterrestrials. The ultimate result of these contacts has been the creation of a remarkable hybrid race — offspring of the combination of human and Grey genetics. This new clan is being integrated into the Universe in a number of locations. Some even reside on the Earth, barely distinguishable from our "pure" human lineage.

It is believed by some abductees and observers of the abductee phenomenon that some of the government agencies who have worked in cooperation with the Greys have their own "abductee programs," which they are using to develop other genetic strains.

AKASHIC RECORDS — A "cosmic diary" of all the knowledge and experiences — past, present, and future — that exist in our Universe. It is an accumulation of individual and group consciousness, literally ALL THAT IS. This information is retained in the eighth dimension and can be accessed by subject or for an individual. When using the Akashic Records to access information "clairvoyantly," it is important to understand that future predictions are based on current circumstances and forces presently at work. With this information, the future can be changed if one so chooses and knows how. The Akashic records update "regularly" to reflect these changes.

ALL THAT IS — The sum total of all individual and group consciousness developed through the experiences of all that exists in our Universe. A record of ALL THAT IS is retained in crystals in the Eighth Dimension (see Akashic Records). ALL THAT IS, is also another name for The Creator.

ASHTAR-EZEKIEL — Ezekiel (not to be confused with the prophet Ezekiel) is the true cosmic name of the entity many on the Earth refer to as Ashtar. Ezekiel is the guardian of the Earth and is responsible for ensuring that the third dimensional "Christ Consciousness" does not leave the Earth until it transitions into the fourth dimension of consciousness. Ezekiel is the cosmic brother of Sananda, that beautiful entity who incarnated on the Earth 2,000 years ago as Jesus Christ. Ezekiel's base of operations is a space station, sometimes referred to as the "mother ship," above the Earth that houses millions of other extraterrestrial beings. It is from this space station that Ezekiel fulfills his responsibility as leader of The Command, composed of millions of beings from a number of planets, star systems, galaxies, and Universes, including our own. Before assuming his responsibility for the Earth and The Command, Ezekiel resided in another Universe.

ASTRAL PLANE — The astral plane should not be confused with the eight dimensions of consciousness. When a being on the

Earth sets aside his or her body and experiences physical death, that being's life force has the choice to proceed through the "portal of death" or into the astral plane. The astral plane is a companion dimension of the Earth. It is this plane of existence that disembodied human incarnates inhabit because they want to continue their close communion with the ways and people of the Earth. Entities who stay here rather than go "to the Light" through the portal of death, do not let go of their human mentality and negative human emotions. Therefore, there is a wide array of consciousness and activity in the astral plane. The phenomenon we refer to as "ghosts" are residents of the astral plane. After a short time here, many of these disembodied entities long to proceed through the portal of death, where the vibrations are much higher and conducive to the life force (see Portal of Death)

ASTRAL TRAVEL — A process whereby a person's life force leaves his or her corporeal body. The life force may stay close to the host body or even travel at length interdimensionally. In some cases, the person maintains conscious memory of the phenomenon after the life force re-enters the body. The name "astral" travel is a misnomer, as such disembodied travel is rarely in the astral plane.

AURA — Our life force is composed of pure energy. When our life force and our human body become partners in the Earth experience, this energy fills our body. The body, however, is not capable of containing ALL the energy of our life force. Our energy, therefore, "spills over" our corporeal boundaries. This creates a halo phenomenon which can be seen extending several inches beyond our human body. We call this phenomenon an "aura." People may see auras as clear, active energy or in a variety of colors.

CHANNEL — A person who serves as a "receiver" of information through paranormal means. The sources of information normally transcend the third dimensional Earth realm but may also include other human beings. It is thought that channels have a vibratory rate that allows them to tap into information, much as a radio taps into frequencies. The life force of a "trance channeler" steps outside his or her body to allow another life force to enter and use the body to impart information. The life force of the "conscious channeler" remains intact in the body and receives information from "outside" sources.

CLAIRVOYANT — Oftentimes called a "psychic," the clairvoyant has the ability to receive information beyond the confines of time, dimension, and space in a variety of ways. This may include channeling, mediumship, and/or empathing. Tools such as playing cards, tarot cards, pendulums, personal objects, items for automatic writing, and scrying mirrors (which Nostradamus reportedly used) may also be utilized to receive and translate information. Although the term "clairvoyant" is used by some in a more limited context to refer to people who are "clear-seeing," clairvoyants can actually receive information in words, feelings, and/or knowingness, as well as through sight perception. The term "clair-audient" refers specifically to people who perceive extraordinary phenomenon through the medium of words and sounds. The term "clair-sentient" designates those who sense and feel extraordinary phenomenon.

CLAN — In our Universe, the inhabitants of the various planets and star systems are known as clans. On Earth, we call ourselves a species. The other residents of the Universe refer to us as the Earthean clan. Likewise, the Pleiadians, Andromedans, Orions, etc. are clans.

CONSCIOUSNESS — The PURPOSE of existence is for all life forces, as individuals and a collective, to grow in consciousness. Consciousness develops through EXPERIENCES. These experiences can manifest in relationships, jobs, education, sports, creative endeavors, and spiritual activities. They are pre-destined to help the person understand himself or herself as a unique individual AND as a citizen of the Universe — not tied to just one planet and its status quo — but with access to ALL THAT IS. The DEPTH of this understanding determines the entity's LEVEL of consciousness.

In human beings, consciousness grows as we integrate our subconscious and supraconscious levels of activity into our CONSCIOUS understanding. The SUB-CONSCIOUS level of our human brain houses memories from our present life that we have "buried." Our SUPRACONSCIOUS level is directly connected to ALL THAT IS, including information from our other lives and information that transcends our present level of consciousness. Our life force, through spiritual activities — such as meditation, contemplation, prayer, compassion, and honesty — can access both the sub-conscious and supra-conscious levels and bring them into our conscious understanding. Our consciousness grows when we honestly LIVE this conscious understanding. When our consciousness grows, the energy vibrations of our life force become higher and lighter.

CORPOREAL BODIES — Bodies of flesh and blood, such as human bodies. These bodies are mortal because their parts literally wear out. These bodies are tools for having experiences in the first through fourth dimensions. Entities who exist in the fifth through eighth dimensions have no need for corporeal bodies and function through their immortal life forces in ethereal bodies. Corporeal bodies are heavier and vibrate at lower rates than ethereal bodies.

COSMIC — Existence beyond the confines of the physical Earth.

COUNCIL OF ELDERS — The leaders of the Pleiadian System. These leaders are neither elected nor appointed. They naturally assume their position on The Council because they have achieved the highest level of consciousness. The

Council and their families reside on the planet Alcyone.

CREATOR, THE — Before anything or anybody else existed, The Creator existed as a complete, self-contained being of pure male and female energy. Because there was only this ONE existence, dynamic growth was impossible. So, the energy of The Creator severed into billions and billions of energetic life forces — all of the universes and everything that exists within those Universes, including our individual life forces. Therefore, The Creator is the origin of ALL THAT IS, the collective of all consciousness. The Creator is a dynamic FORCE — not a person, but a *personality* — the personality of the whole, of ALL THAT IS.

All of the life forces that The Creator gave birth to became creators, as well. Each of these creators had all of the characteristics of The Source Creator. The Creator commissioned these creators to go out together and create more of existence, to experience that existence, and to develop greater vibrations as a result of those experiences. This book refers to these progeny of The Creator as co-creators. You are a co-creator.

The Creator is often confused with the human concept called "God." See the definition of "God" for an explanation of the difference between the two.

DIMENSION — The level of awareness or consciousness which an entity has achieved. The reality of the entity is determined by this level of consciousness and the vibrations of the energy within this consciousness. There are eight dimensions of consciousness within our Universe, with a number of different levels of accomplishment and ability within each dimension. The Earth and its inhabitants have passed through the first two dimensions of consciousness and now reside within the third dimensional consciousness. Our TRANSITION into the fourth dimension of consciousness is now in process. The eighth dimension is home to ALL

THAT IS and those most highly evolved in consciousness within our Universe.

DUALITY — The primary challenge and opportunity of the third dimensional consciousness is to experience the opposites and opposition in all things. For example, sickness and health, happiness and sorrow, fear and freedom, love and hate. These opposites — duality — arise from the co-existence of our mortal body with our immortal life force. Our negotiations with duality afford us the opportunity to make choices and exercise our free will. The intended outcome of these negotiations is the manifestation of balance and higher consciousness. Another word for duality is "polarity."

EGO — Our life forces know their nature is divine. They like themselves. They love themselves. They know that existence is simply an OPPORTUNITY to grow in consciousness. They also know that beyond our third dimensional corporeal Earth consciousness there is no "higher" judgment of how we deal with these opportunities. Here on the Earth, however, judgment is rampant. It shoots "holes in our hearts." We begin to forget our divinity and stop liking ourselves. When a true love supply is not available to us, we sometimes fill those holes in our hearts with ARTIFICIAL self-esteem. This artificial self-esteem is called "ego." Ego is actually a lower level vibration that tells us in order to feel good about ourselves, we have to diminish or disempower others. We do this by complaining, criticizing, condemning, and attempting to control others.

EMPATH — Someone capable of experiencing the thoughts and feelings of another living or deceased being (see Medium).

ENERGY — The true nature of all of existence, including The Creator and the individual co-creators. Energy vibrates at different "levels." Our reality is determined by the level of vibrations we are experiencing within our individual life force and within the dimension of consciousness we reside.

We literally travel into other dimensions on the back of vibrations. Thought is a vibration, unconditional love is a vibration, consciousness is a vibration — everything you experience is a vibration of energy.

ENTITIES — All life forms in the Universe, including human.

ETHEREAL BODY — The composition of ethereal bodies is energy that vibrates at a higher level than corporeal matter. Some entities, using higher vibrations than the corporeal, can create forms that appear to be corporeal even though they are not of flesh and blood. They can also create other vehicles for experience that take any form they choose. The Pleiadians, who work with this "liquid energy," are called "shape shifters" because they have the capability of assuming many forms.

ETHEREAL REALMS — Dimensions of consciousness that are not composed of corporeal matter. Entities and planetary systems in the fifth through the eighth dimensions exist in the ethereal realms. The first through the fourth dimensions, which includes the third dimensional Earth, are in the corporeal realms.

EXTRATERRESTRIAL — A noun or adjective used to describe anything or any entity that does not reside within the third dimensional Earth consciousness.

EZEKIEL-ASHTAR — Ezekiel is the true cosmic name of the entity many on the Earth refer to as Ashtar. See "Ashtar-Ezekiel" for an expanded description of this blessed entity.

GAIA — The cosmic name of the Earth. Gaia (pronounced guy-a) is an entity who attained a state of pure knowledge and integrity and then chose to become a planet on which other entities could work their way to achieving this same state.

GOD — The human concept of God was encoded in the human genetic DNA by the architects of the mortal, corporeal body of the "human" species. These architects were not from the Earth; rather they were from another clan in the Universe.

Just as humans pioneer new territory on the Earth, it is the custom of the Universe for its citizens to pioneer new planets. For this reason, this extraterrestrial clan came to the Earth with genetically engineered bodies to serve as vehicles for experiencing life on our planet. They genetically coded our human brain to view them as our creators, and we subsequently named them "gods." We then created a definition of our gods to include their responsibility to protect, nurture, teach, and respond to us. When other clans visited us "from the heavens," we called them gods, too. Through time, some aspects of our human civilization whittled our gods down to one almighty, all-seeing, omnipotent god who demanded our homage and strict obedience, using guilt, shame, and fear to keep us in line. In fact, our gods were simply extraterrestrial beings, not unlike ourselves. When we can accept the fact that we are not our bodies — that our bodies are simply vehicles for experiencing existence in the first through fourth dimensions of consciousness — then we can understand our connection to that which we call the "divine." Freed from the boundaries of our human brains, our true, immortal self — our life force — knows that which we long for, that which is our origin, that which we are bonded to immortally is The Creator (see The Creator).

GUIDE — An entity from another dimension, oftentimes unseen but either heard or "felt," who serves us as a teacher of higher consciousness. A guide always has a specific purpose to accomplish. This may be an entity of our own choosing before our incarnation, or an entity who has chosen to serve us because of his or her particular abilities or goals.

HUMAN INCARNATE — Any entity who has had three or more consecutive (re)incarnations upon the Earth and, thereby, becomes bound to the Earth's dimension of consciousness. Some human incarnates were once Starseed who chose to continue reincarnating upon the Earth for their own personal reasons — service to humanity or an ongoing relationship with a human incarnate, for example (see Starseed).

LIFE FORCE — Sometimes referred to as our "higher self," our life force is our true, immortal, pure-energy self. As an offspring of The Creator, our life force is connected by cosmic DNA to ALL THAT IS. These cosmic genetics also relate us to ALL other life forces in our Universe. When we begin the "dance of life" with our human body on Earth, our life force envelops our human body in its bosom — to lead and guide us through our human experiences into a state of higher consciousness. If we forget we are our life force and not our human body, life experiences challenge us to remember who we REALLY are.

LIGHT BODY — Another name for ethereal body.

LOST TIME — A phenomenon experienced by some people who have had contact with extraterrestrial beings. Basically, this refers to the fact that most human beings who have extraterrestrial contact do not have CONSCIOUS recall of these incidents. As a result, a person may look at his or her watch at 9:00 p.m. and five minutes later the watch will read 11:00 p.m. In actuality, two hours have passed that the person does not consciously remember.

MEDIUM — A person who has the ability to empath with human beings who have experienced the death of their corporeal bodies and have not yet reincarnated on the Earth plane. These entities, who no longer have corporeal bodies, exist either in the astral plane or have gone "to the Light" through the portal of death (see Astral Plane and Portal of Death). Medium communications can include seeing, hearing, and experiencing the feelings of the disincarnated entity.

MERKABAH — The "ultimate" vehicle, the merkabah is composed of pure energy and transports the occupant through time, dimension, and space at "warp" speed. It creates an energy zone around the (ethereal) body that looks like a bubble of light. In the Universe, it is sometimes referred to as a "tube of light." The Merkabah can be created in a variety of ways, but only entities who function without ego are capable of using it to travel through interdimensional portals. The picture on the first page of this book contains an actual photograph of Zachary (see Zachary) in a merkabah bubble.

MIND — This refers to the UNIVERSAL MIND, not the human brain. The Universal Mind is the realm of the life force. It is here that the collective consciousness — ALL THAT IS — exists and can be accessed through the Akashic Records. Clairvoyants "tap into" the Universal Mind to receive information from the past, present, future, and other dimensions.

MISSION — The responsibility and opportunity that drives every Starseed upon the Earth. Every Starseed now upon the Earth has the mission to assist in the TRANSITION of the Earth into the fourth dimension of consciousness. Most Starseed have also volunteered to fulfill another mission for the Earth and its inhabitants. Missions include a wide variety of activities directly related to the origin or abilities of the individual Starseed — bringing and teaching higher consciousness, creative art and music, healing, balanced male and female energy, and advanced technology, to name but a few.

MOTHER SHIP — The Command's base of operations (see The Command). A very large space station that is home to millions of extraterrestrials in service to the Earth. These extraterrestrials are from a variety of clans from our own galaxy, other galaxies, and even other universes. Life on the mother ship includes lively operating activities, as well as the personal activities of the unique and varied individuals who reside there.

MULTI-DIMENSIONAL TRAVEL — The activity of by-passing the human brain to walk and function in other dimensions of consciousness (there are eight dimensions of consciousness with different levels of accomplishment and ability within each dimension). These dimensions include places, times, and "lifestyles" beyond present human comprehension. Movement beyond the present human plane can take place through the process of astral travel or traveling the Universal Mind (see Astral Travel and Mind). Traveling the Universal Mind requires an altered state of consciousness and can be accomplished with the assistance of guides, angels, extraterrestrials, and other transcendent beings. Entities of higher dimensional consciousness can travel the lower dimensions without assistance. Physical space craft can only maneuver in the dimensions which have vibrations similar to the composition of the space craft.

OVERSOUL — Just as The Creator's life force energy severed into myriads of co-creators — to overcome the "limitations of one" — likewise, our own individual life force may have severed into a number of other expressions of our self. Our oversouls can exist simultaneously in other times and dimensions. They can also manifest simultaneously in the same time and dimension. The purpose of having oversouls is to "make the most" of our unique existence. The experiences and learnings of one oversoul become part of the consciousness of all of the other oversouls. Just as we are related to The Creator, we are uniquely tied to our oversouls through cosmic DNA. We oftentimes connect with our oversouls through the dream state.

PLEIADES — A star system with over two hundred planets ranging from the fourth through the eighth dimensions of consciousness. The Pleiadians have been involved with the Earth and its inhabitants for many thousands of years. Our history and cultures reflect their many contributions to Earthean civilization. The Pleiadians are similar in appearance to human beings, although those in the fifth through the eight dimensions of consciousness manifest form through their ethereal bodies. There are many Starseed from the Pleiades, now upon the Earth, who have come here to help in the TRANSITION into the fourth dimension.

PORTAL — A doorway between two dimensions. As the vibrations on either side of the portal are very different, the vibrations of the portal have to allow for safe passage between the two dimensions. Therefore, portals are distinguishable by their animated and "unusual" vibrations.

PORTAL OF DEATH — A dimensional portal through which the life forces of human beings who experience the death of their corporeal bodies pass into the experience of "life" without a mortal human body and negative human emotions. It is this portal that many humans who have had near death experiences describe as a "tunnel leading to a bright light." All humans who pass through the portal of death are accompanied by loving guides into a realm of lighter, higher vibrations and non-judgment. This is a "companion realm" to the Earth where disincarnated humans have the opportunity to access the BIG PICTURE of existence and remember their relationship to the entire Universe. Based on this greater understanding, they determine what they want to accomplish in their next incarnation and can even pre-ordain relationships and experiences.

PRAYER — Prayer is a two-way communication system that has existed since the beginning of creation. Prayer was part of THE PLAN of The Creator and the co-creators to have all of us stay connected to one another. Through this communication system, we are capable of communicating with The Creator and with one another over long distances, even insofar as between planets. Prayer is closely related to those processes that we on Earth call "channeling" and "interdimensional travel." It is also akin to that process we call "empathing," whereby we can know what is happening with somebody at extraordinary distances. Prayer is significant only when it comes from the true essence of the entity communicating it. The most appropriate content and form of prayer reaches out honestly, creates the clearest link of communication, and generates the strongest feeling of unconditional love.

PURPOSE — All human incarnates, after passing through the portal of death, pre-determine for themselves a purpose in their next incarnation. These purposes are as varied as the entities who choose them. Human beings will continue their search for purpose during their incarnation until recalling and manifesting these self-made commitments.

QUICKENING — A dramatic opening of spiritual consciousness in the CONSCIOUS level of one's human brain. This is accomplished by the raising of vibrations within the human body by the body's pure-energy life force. The quickening person often experiences significant revelations into the deeper meaning of existence and a connection with all of universal existence. As a result, the person can feel "unnerved," experiencing tremors, shaking, and an all-around sense of disconnection with his or her former reality. This initial state of "shock" usually wears off within a matter of hours or days. Then the person can revel in his or her newfound connection with ALL THAT IS. This is what everyone will experience at some point during the TRANSITION into the fourth dimensional consciousness.

REALITY — Our reality is based upon the dimension of consciousness we have attained. That reality is our classroom. What we are to learn in that classroom is what is MISSING in our reality — aspects of the fullest understanding of our self and our relationship to the rest of our Universe. Our course work is EXPERIENCES that challenge us to this greater understanding. When we work our way up through the first seven grades (or dimensions) and arrive at the eighth grade/dimension, we will know What Really Is. For in this eighth dimension, we will find the collective of ALL experience and knowledge— The Creator — also known as ALL THAT IS.

REINCARNATION — Like The Creator, we co-creators are immortal. Our journey in existence is to have experiences that guide us into greater awareness and, thereby, higher dimensions of consciousness. The Universal Plan provides for our life forces to have these experiences in the first four dimensions of consciousness in vehicles of mortal, CORPOREAL bodies. When our corporeal bodies are terminally exhausted, our life forces join with new bodies so our journey will not be interrupted. We refer to this process of recycling life forces into new corporeal bodies as reincarnation. A specific reincarnation is referred to as an "incarnation."

In the fifth through eighth dimensions, reincarnation does not involve corporeal bodies. Entities in these dimensions incarnate into different PURPOSES, sometimes in a newborn manifestation, sometimes in an adult manifestation. These manifestations are in the form of ethereal bodies (see Ethereal Body).

SANANDA — The cosmic name of the entity known as Jesus Christ. Sananda manifested upon the Earth two thousand years ago as part of the TRANSITION from the second to the third dimensional (Christ) consciousness. This plan to raise the Earth to the third dimensional consciousness was formulated by Sananda's cosmic father. It was also part of this plan — and subsequently agreed between Sananda and his cosmic brother, Ezekiel — that Sananda would help establish this third dimensional consciousness upon the Earth and Ezekiel would serve as its guardian.

SOUL EXCHANGE — Human bodies are the vehicle of our third dimensional consciousness. Sometimes, the life force that fuels a human body chooses to leave for personal reasons. If the body is intact, it is sometimes more appropriate to gift the body to another life force rather than end its existence. The change from one life force to another is called a soul exchange. A soul exchange is always done with the permission of the original life force. Depending upon the circumstances of the departing life force, the process can take place in a number of hours or may take a number of years. The new life force is sometimes referred to as a "walk-in." A walk-in is an oversoul of the life force that wishes to depart (see Oversoul).

SOUL GROUP — Before human incarnates reincarnate upon the Earth, they pre-determine many of their life experiences. Part of planning these life experiences is choosing the other life forces who will participate in them. Those life forces who choose to come together to create experiences and, thereby, produce opportunities for growth in consciousness are part of a soul group. The "members" of a soul group are sometimes referred to as "soul mates."

SPIRITUALITY — Spirituality is the eternal path of the life force. As we never arrive, it is the journey and not the destination that is key to an entity's spiritual transformation. As The Creator has told us, "There is always MORE" — to learn, experience, savor, and share. Even eighth dimensional entities continue to experience transformation . . . *there is always a god's god.* For, when we have learned all that we can within our Universe, we can move into the experiences of other universes.

In the third dimensional consciousness, spirituality is, in part, learning to deal with time. The things that matter are timeless — the life force, integrity, love, transformation, and the beauty of character.

STARSEED — Life forces who come from other planets, star systems, galaxies, and even other universes with a specific mission to help the Earth and its human inhabitants. Starseed are either born into human bodies or enter a human body "midstream" in the body's incarnation through a soul exchange. Starseed presently upon the Earth now number about ten thousand. All these Starseed are here to assist the Earth and its inhabitants through the TRANSITION into the fourth dimension, as well as to fulfill missions unique to their individual talents and abilities.

THE COMMAND — In terms of dimensional consciousness, the Earth is as a child. To ensure the Earth's protection from other elements that might cause confusion and upset this level of consciousness, a guardian for the Earth was appointed by the Spiritual Forces of the Universe. This guardianship is accomplished by millions of extraterrestrial (non-Earth) entities who function as The Command. Most recently, responsibility of The Command was assumed by Ezekiel, the cosmic brother of Sananda. Ezekiel assumed responsibility of The Command when Sananda incarnated on the Earth as Jesus Christ to raise the Earth from the second to the third dimension of (Christ) consciousness. At that time, Ezekiel assumed guardianship for the Earth and its third dimensional consciousness.

TIME — In the third dimensional Earth consciousness, time is viewed as being LINEAR. That is, we equate time with the existence of the human body — having a beginning and an end. Linear time exists in our third dimensional consciousness so human beings can experience duality and, therefore, differences (see Duality). In the higher dimensions of our Universe, time is observed from the viewpoint of the immortal life force. Therefore, it is not viewed as being linear. Rather, existence evolves appropriately in the context of APPROPRIATE TIME. In reality, past, present, and future are occurring SIMULTANEOUSLY, not linearly. This can be better understood by comparing time to a compact disc. For example, from one music CD, a person can select a specific song from a variety of songs. Likewise, from the "time CD" entitled *Past, Present & Future,* a person can choose a specific track, or "space in time." The selected "time" track will provide the person with a variety of experiences (feelings and emotions) linked to the consciousness, activities, and opportunities of that space in time.

TRANSCENDENTS — The three primary Transcendents referred to in this book are named Zachary, Sananda, and Ezekiel. They are referred to as Transcendents because their consciousness transcends the third dimensional consciousness in which the Earth resides. These particular Transcendents are residents of the eighth dimension — the highest dimension of consciousness in our Universe. These extraordinary entities have worked tirelessly with the Earth and its inhabitants as teachers, guardians, and spiritual leaders. They presently communicate through the channel, Janis Abriel, sharing their transcendent wisdom — which is being shared with you in this book. For more information on these unique and enlightened entities, refer to the chapter entitled "Finding the Starseed."

TRANSITION INTO THE FOURTH DIMENSION — The inhabitants of the Earth have currently achieved the third dimension of consciousness (see Dimension). Our TRANSITION into the fourth dimension of consciousness is now in process. This TRANSITION involves dramatic physical and spiritual changes in the Earth and its inhabitants. A more comprehensive description of this TRANSITION and what it entails can be found in the chapter entitled "The Fourth Dimension."

TUBES OF LIGHT — (See Merkabah.)

UNIVERSAL MIND — (See Mind.)

UNIVERSE — Our Universe is a dynamic SYSTEM of existence. This system is home to eight dimensions of consciousness and myriads of planets, star systems, and galaxies teeming with sentient life and activity. When we become fearless enough to look beyond our LITTLE PICTURE of existence here on the Earth, we can actively step into this BIG PICTURE of the Universe. Seeing ourselves as universal citizens, we can begin to comprehend the magnitude of the opportunities that await us — travel to other planets, dimensions, and times; relationships with other clans (species); knowledge and technology beyond our present comprehension; riding the vibrations of higher consciousness to experiences of unconditional love and joy — just to name a few. Then we can begin pondering the opportunities available to us when we are competent to enter other universes with their own unique dimensions of consciousness and activity.

VIBRATION — To say "It's all in the vibration," is to put existence in a nutshell. The nature of existence is energy. The QUALITY of existence is the level of VIBRATION of that energy. Our form is a vibration. Thought, unconditional love, and joy are vibrations. In fact, our entire reality is a vibration. We literally travel into other dimensions on the back of such vibrations. The true masters of the Universe are masters of energy and their vibrations.

WALK-IN — Another name for someone who has accomplished a soul exchange (see Soul Exchange).

WORLD GOVERNMENT — An extremely powerful, usually unseen group of people who manipulate world issues from "behind the scenes." This group stands more powerful than the combination of individual governments in determining the outcome of issues on planet Earth. Other names for this group are "secret government," "shadow government," and "the Illuminati." These people use their power ruthlessly to serve their own selfish, materialistic interests. Their activities do not represent the best interests of humanity.

ZACHARY — The alpha and omega of this book, Zachary has been Janis Abriel's companion, teacher, mentor, and guide through multiple dimensions since 1993. He is also Jan's

Pleiadian father. Zachary is an eighth dimensional entity from the planet Alcyone in the Pleiadian star system. He serves there on the Pleiadian Council of Elders as a leader and diplomat. Though he travels the Universe extensively, his present mission is in service to the Earth and its TRANSITION into the fourth dimension of consciousness. His eight Pleiadian children are also in service to the Earth.